PRESERVED
STEAM-POWERED
MACHINES

JOHN HANNAVY

First published in Great Britain in 2012

Written and photographed by John Hannavy.
Copyright © John Hannavy 2012
www.johnhannavy.co.uk

British Library Cataloguing-in-Publication Data
A CIP record for this title is available from the
British Library

ISBN 978 0 85710 072 6

PiXZ Books
Halsgrove House, Ryelands Business Park,
Bagley Road, Wellington, Somerset TA21 9PZ
Tel: 01823 653777
Fax: 01823 216796
email: sales@halsgrove.com

Front cover image: Cornishman was built by Garrett in Leiston, Suffolk, in 1912 carrying Works
No.30959. It was supplied new to John Griffiths of Bargoed in Glamorgan but was later converted
into a road-roller. It was returned to its original specification during restoration. *Back Cover image:*
The replica of Thomas Guppy and Isambard Kingdom Brunel's massive 4-cylinder low pressure
engine which powered SS *Great Britain*. The replica engine, although driven by electricity, gives
a unique opportunity to see the workings of a maritime engine design from the early 1840s, and
the chain drive which powered the propeller of the world's first screw-driven passenger liner.

Title page image: The top-hatted driver of Wigan Coal & Iron Company's 1887-built 0-6-0ST
Lindsay looks for the guard's green flag before pulling away from the platform at Steamtown,
Carnforth, on the occasion of Lindsay's centenary celebrations. She is still operational, but
currently stored at the West Coast Railway Company's sheds at Carnforth, Lancashire.

Contents page image: Full speed ahead and going nowhere! The engine telegraph on the bridge
of the 1901-built RRS *Discovery* in her permanent dry dock in Dundee. The decision to
build *Discovery* at Dundee was made on account of the port's long experience of building whaling
ships with hulls sufficiently strong to withstand the ice and conditions she was going to
experience in the Antarctic.

CONTENTS

PREFACE

This book does not set out to be a history of steam – rather it is a look at steam today, with a few backward glances through old photographs where appropriate. Photography has been around for a little more than 170 years, but not all historic photographs are necessarily old. History sometimes happened only yesterday, and some of the steam machines I photographed years ago have been radically overhauled and repainted as comparison pictures illustrate – and that makes my earlier images part of the on-going visual history of preserved steam powered machines.

We are now well into the second generation of people born since steam locomotives were withdrawn from Britain's railways in the 1960s, yet small children today are almost as familiar with the sounds and smells of steam engines as I was more than sixty years ago.

Crowded station platforms on 'Thomas' days are regular proof of the enduring fascination of steam.

Today there are over 1300 preserved steam railway locomotives operating in Britain alone, and countless others operating successfully on heritage lines across the world!

Opposite: The driver of Beamish Open Air Museum's recreation of John Buddle and William Chapman's 1815 'Steam Elephant' takes a rest.

Below: The author at the controls of GWR 0-6-0ST No.813 on the East Somerset Railway in 2008. Built by Hudswell Clarke & Co in Leeds in 1901 for the Port Talbot Railway, 813 passed into GWR ownership in 1923, was sold in 1934 for use in north-east collieries, and was purchased for preservation in 1966. The locomotive is now based at the Severn Valley Railway in Shropshire.

Britain's locomotive industry was so successful in the 19th and early 20th centuries that many of the preserved steam trains operating in what were the far-flung corners of Empire were originally built in Newcastle, or Glasgow.

But simply preserving these behemoths is not enough. Unless we can see, hear and smell them at work, they are no more than curios, museum pieces.

But in steam – railway or road engine, industrial engine or steamboat – these machines come alive. And for a price, you can even take the controls of a locomotive, or even a paddle steamer, yourself. Whoever thought steam would die out?

Over the fifty-plus years during which I have been taking photographs, the heritage scene has expanded beyond measure. The popularity of steam fairs, preserved mill engines, steamboats, and railways seems to know no limits. Steam heritage is now big business, a major employer, and a hugely enjoyable part of our leisure time.

This book celebrates more than a century and a half of steam preservation in Britain – some of it successful, some of it, sadly, doomed to failure.

John Hannavy, 2012

Opposite: Steam preservation now has a worldwide following. Here a lorry is loading coal on to the steamer TSS *Earnslaw* at Queenstown on Lake Wakatipu on New Zealand's South Island. To counteract the increased weight on one side of the 100-year old steamer, a two-ton concrete block is moved across the deck!

Inset: Keith Simpson at the controls of the Kingston Flyer on New Zealand's South Island. He has driven steam trains all over the world - including in Britain - but the 'Flyer' is his first love. NZR locomotive 778 - built in 1925 as No.235 - operates a heritage line south of Queenstown. A century ago, the Kingston Flyer service used to connect with the TSS *Earnslaw* at the south end of Lake Wakatipu, an early integrated transport system.

Left: The preserved steam engine at New Lanark was rescued from a former weaving mill in Selkirk. New Lanark's original steam engine which provided ancillary power had been removed long before the mills - now a World Heritage Site - were even considered for preservation.

INTRODUCTION

It is impossible to overstate the importance of steam in driving industrial Britain. When steam power started to replace water power in mills and factories, production soared – steam-power was reliable and available twenty-four hours a day, whereas waterwheels only turned and worked the machinery when there was a lot of water in the river which fed the wheel. In Victorian Britain, the steam engine was almost ubiquitous, powering mills, factories, sawmills, forges and foundries, mines, railways, and ships and boats.

Britain's dependence on coal was almost total, and tens of millions of tons of the stuff were burned each year to keep the factory wheels turning, and to keep transport on the move.

Despite the fact that water power had been, in effect, free, the demand for ever-greater productivity and profit meant that the considerable investment required to convert a factory

Above: Steam-powered machinery at Stott Park Bobbin Mill, Cumbria was fuelled by burning the mill's wood waste.

Opposite top: PS *Lord of the Isles* at Inveraray Pier c.1890. This photograph was published as a postcard c.1904.

Opposite bottom: A narrow-gauge steam railway in use to transport boilers at Horwich locomotive works, 1904.

to steam, and the on-going cost of fuelling the engines, was entirely worthwhile.

It was the same in every industry – the running costs were easily met by increased profits and, in turn, the increasing success of the large mills and factories led to the creation of more jobs.

The development of the railway networks, and of coastal steamer services made it possible for the population to increase its mobility. That in turn – combined with statutory holidays – drove the expansion of many coastal resorts into mass holiday venues. When the mills closed for a week, railways were standing by ready to take the workers in their tens of thousands to resorts like Blackpool, Clacton, Brighton and Tynemouth.

Steamer services connected London with the resorts along the south and east coast: Blackpool with North Wales; Glasgow with Scotland's west coast and islands. Indeed, long before there was a railway line across the Scottish border, steamer services were already the well-established route north. Leaving the railway train behind at Fleetwood on the Lancashire coast, visitors to Scotland had an often-stormy sail

Opposite: Flying the flag - gleaming paintwork, shining brass, and proudly on display.

The remarkable thing about steam heritage is that most of the work is done by volunteers, including occasionally the author, below. The economics of operating a steam railway, a steamboat, or a road engine are such that what money there is goes on restoration, preservation and operation. Only on a very few of the most successful heritage projects are there many paid staff. On most steam projects, almost all the operational work is carried out by enthusiasts happy to give up weekends and holidays for the sheer delight of getting filthy and being embraced by that wonderful smell. Not everyone can be a train driver, but there is great pleasure to be got out of working at any one of the many jobs around the yard. Even young volunteers are being drawn by the allure of steam.

to Ardrossan on the Clyde coast, followed by a train journey to Glasgow.

Demand for ever-larger and ever greater power led to some remarkable developments in steam engine design. Improved boiler design greatly improved efficiency, and improved engineering turned the once unreliable steam engine into an entirely reliable and fuel-efficient workhorse. But in an age of plentiful coal supplies, cheap labour, and an often total disregard for health and safety, there was never any likelihood of a shortage of fuel or men to mine it.

Inevitably, redundant steam locomotives and steam ships were scrapped without sentimentality once their operational life was at an end. The survival of so many steam-powered machines today is a mixture of luck – in that no-one got round to breaking them up – and sheer dogged determination.

Steam reigned supreme for over 150 years before cheaper and cleaner power sources displaced it. But the demise of the steam age has left us with some wonderful machines, many in museums, but just as many still periodically breathing and belching steam and smoke. This book is their story.

Left top: Black 5 45428 prepares to depart from Pickering. Built by Armstrong Whitworth in Newcastle in 1937, the Stanier-designed locomotive is now named *Eric Treacy*. Ten Black 5s are still operational.

Below left: SS *Simla* herself may be gone, but a model of her steam engine is on display in Glasgow's new Riverside Transport Museum.

Below: Seen here in Leith Docks in 1972, HMS *Dolphin*, an 1882 steam frigate, survived for 95 years before being broken up in 1977.

STEAMBOATS and STEAMSHIPS

Given the manner in which history has dealt with the first steam railway – almost everyone has heard of the Stockton & Darlington Railway – the early history of the steam boat is much less well-known. While every important railway anniversary has been celebrated with ceremonies, cavalcades, and ever-wider media coverage, anniversaries of the short journey undertaken by the world's first steam-powered boat have gone unnoticed except by a few. The place was Dalswinton Loch near Dumfries, and the date was October 14, 1788, so both the centenary and bi-centenary have both long passed, and passed unfeted.

The boat was a pleasure craft, which had been fitted with a modified Watt steam engine by William Symington, a Lanarkshire engineer. Accounts differ on the success or otherwise of the experiment – some accounts say the vessel achieved a speed of 5mph for a time – but the short journey the boat made demonstrated the viability of steam power on water.

Opposite: RRS *Discovery* is now permanently displayed in drydock in Dundee, the port in which she was built. In preservation, she carries Port Stanley as her port of registration, in recognition of the large part of her working life she spent in the South Atlantic

Below: The engines from RRS *Discovery* were sold for scrap long ago, so all that visitors to Dundee see today is a model.

Right: The hull interior of Brunel's SS *Great Britain* in the early 1980s, a large empty space in the process of being strengthened. This was one of the early stages in restoring the hulk rescued from the Falklands back to the appearance Brunel himself would have recognised. Sadly, her 35 years open to the elements in Bristol from 1970 until 2005 caused greater deterioration to the hull than her 125 years at sea.

Below: Brunel's 1859-built, 32,000 ton, SS *Great Eastern*, seen here off Southampton in a stereoscopic, 3D, view by the George Washington Wilson studio in the early 1860s. The development of massive steamships provoked a lot of public attention.

The Cattle Pier,
Balaklava, 1855
during the Crimean
War. The mixture of
sail and steam ships
packed into the little
harbour reflects the
navy's growing use of
steam or auxiliary-
steam power.

HMS *Warrior* entered
Royal Navy service in
1860 and is Britain's
oldest-surviving
steam-powered
warship. She is
preserved as part of
the Historic Ships
Collection in
Portsmouth Docks.

Right: *Gondola's* engine room photographed in 2009, with her second new boiler painted in Furness Railway Company colours.

Below: The engine room of the steam yacht *Gondola* as it looked in the 1980s just a few years after it was returned to service by The National Trust.

Usually recognised as the world's first working steamboat, the *Charlotte Dundas* was a paddle steamer built by Alexander Hart at Grangemouth to Symington's design, with his powerful vertical cylinder engine driving the paddle wheels. The boat was successfully demonstrated on the Forth & Clyde Canal in January 1803.

With the steam engine having been invented in Scotland – by James Watt – it is perhaps not entirely surprising that much of the early experimentation on steamboats was carried out north of the border. But others were also at work in France and the United States. France's first steamer sailed along the Seine, and then apparently sank!

America introduced the world's first passenger-carrying steamboat service in 1807, the *North River Steamboat*, later renamed *Clermont*, operating a service between New York and Albany

Back in Scotland, an early promoter of steamships was one Henry Bell who, as early as 1803 had been urging the Admiralty to consider steam power for their river and sea-going vessels. Despite his ideas being enthusiastically recommended by none other than Lord Nelson, who told the

The owners of Ullswater's 1877-built *Lady of the Lake* believe she is the oldest working passenger vessel in the world - *Gondola* was built as a private steam yacht, and never originally intended for passenger service. *Lady of the Lake* was built in Glasgow by Thomas B Seath & Company of Rutherglen, and transported to Ullswater in sections for reassembly at the waterside. Along with her sister *Raven*, and Windermere's cargo steamer *Raven* they are the only three working survivors of more than 300 vessels turned out by the Rutherglen yard. No longer steam-powered, *Lady of the Lake* was converted to deisel in 1936.

The steam yacht *Gondola*, seen here in 2010, was built for the Furness Railway in 1859, and still sails Coniston Water regularly today. Taken out of service in 1936, she was converted into a houseboat. In the 1960s, she was partially sunk in a storm, and abandoned for over a decade. When salvaged, the original hull was found to be virtually beyond repair, and she was completely rebuilt at Vickers in Barrow, returning to service in 1980.

Sea Lords "if you do not adopt Mr Bell's scheme, other nations will, and in the end vex every vein of this Empire", Bell's ideas remained no more than just ideas. Until 1812, that is. By then Henry Bell and his wife had moved to Helensburgh of the Firth of Clyde where she had taken the post of superintendent of the public baths in 1808.

Bell's steamboat *Comet* was built for him by John Wood & Co of Port Glasgow, and delivered in early 1812. When Bell introduced a thrice-weekly service between Glasgow, Greenock and Helensburgh, *Comet* became the first of generations of Clyde paddle-steamers which worked the river over the following century and a half. Her speed was a mere 5mph!

The rise of steam navigation was rapid. In August 1826, less than fifteen years after Bell's fragile craft had introduced the first passenger steam services in Europe, the *Inverness Courier* newspaper carried an account of the first passenger steamship to sail round the north of Scotland.

A tiny steamer, the SS *United Kingdom* sailed from Glasgow, through the Hebrides, round Cape Wrath, up to Orkney, south again to Wick, Aberdeen and Newhaven on the Firth of Forth. Stories of early steamships belching smoke as they made their way slowly along the north west coast of Scotland were sometimes reported in contemporary newspaper accounts as being 'ships on fire'!

The steam launch *Swallow*, built in 1860, giving visitors a first-hand experience of sailing on the lake – including the pleasure of a cup of tea brewed directly from the boiler! She is seen here returning to the Windermere Steamboat Museum's jetty in 2004.

The passenger steamer *Tern* and cargo boat *Raven* at Lakeside Pier, Windermere, from a 1904 postcard.

While fragile craft were negotiating Britain's coastal waters, by the middle of the 19th century steam power was being developed inland, on canals, rivers, lakes and lochs. And not just for commerce – pleasure steamers were being built for England's larger lakes, and Scotland's major lochs. The steamer SS *Lady of the Lake* was introduced on to Windermere in 1845, followed five years later by the rather Scottish-sounding *Lord of the Isles*. In 1851 *Fire Fly* was launched to operate a rival service, followed a year later by *Dragon Fly*.

Just a few miles away, SY *Gondola*, still sailing today under National Trust ownership, was launched on to Coniston Water in 1859.

Sharing the waters with these passenger-carrying vessels, a profusion of small private pleasure steamers were built for the wealthy lakeside landowners.

On Loch Lomond, the first steamer was David Napier's *Marian*, brought to the loch as an experiment in 1818, just six years after *Comet's* pioneering service had been introduced on the Clyde. Not everyone was happy.

Lord Jeffrey, later to become Lord Advocate, remarked "It is a new experiment for the temptation of tourists. It circumnavigates the whole lake in about ten hours and it was certainly strange and striking to hear and see it hissing and roaring past the headlands of our little bay, foaming and shouting like an angry whale, but on the whole it rather vulgarises the scene too much, and I am glad that it is found not to answer, and has to be dropped next year." She wasn't dropped, and actually encouraged rivals!

The introduction of steam on to Loch Katrine in the Trossachs came much later, but made headlines! The small paddle steamer *Gypsy* was launched on to the waters in 1843, but she didn't last long. One night that same year, the steamer simply disappeared, and has never been found! The oarsmen she had

SS *Rob Roy*, entered service on Loch Katrine in 1856 and worked the loch until withdrawn in 1901.

Passengers are going on board the steamer *La Marguerite* at Llandudno for the return trip to Liverpool. *La Marguerite* had been built in 1894 for the Tilbury to Boulogne cross-Channel service, but proved expensive to run, so was sold for use between Liverpool and the Menai Bridge where coal and wages were a lot cheaper! She was withdrawn from service in 1925.

made redundant were suspected of sending her to the bottom of the loch, and were taken to court.

But refusing to speak English – their Gaelic was apparently un-translatable – the court case descended into farce, and a verdict was returned that the paddler has been sunk by persons or objects unknown! Steamers, clearly, were not universally popular!

By 1845 a new vessel had been launched – the first of two to be named *Rob Roy*, and it this vessel carried the first party of tourists brought to the Trossachs by Thomas Cook in 1846. This was a period when tourism was in the ascendancy – thanks to improved steamer and railway links with England and with the major population centres in Scotland itself. So relatively quickly, a third and larger steamer was commissioned and, also named *Rob Roy*, entered service in 1856. No photographs of the first *Rob Roy* seem to have survived – given the primitive capabilities of photography at the time, perhaps few were taken.

However the second and larger steamer to carry the name was photographed often during her 45-year life on the loch. Throughout

Raven was built for the Furness Railway in 1871, and now is the only vessel preserved on Windermere to be built for commerce rather than leisure.

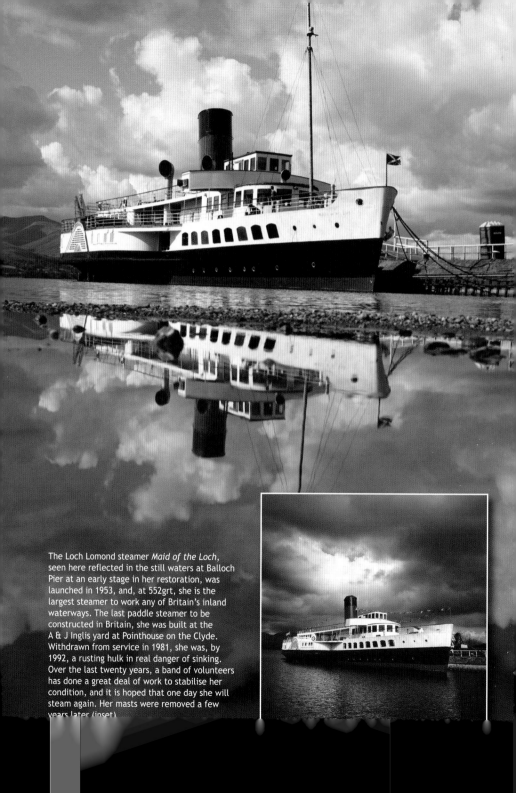

The Loch Lomond steamer *Maid of the Loch*, seen here reflected in the still waters at Balloch Pier at an early stage in her restoration, was launched in 1953, and, at 552grt, she is the largest steamer to work any of Britain's inland waterways. The last paddle steamer to be constructed in Britain, she was built at the A & J Inglis yard at Pointhouse on the Clyde. Withdrawn from service in 1981, she was, by 1992, a rusting hulk in real danger of sinking. Over the last twenty years, a band of volunteers has done a great deal of work to stabilise her condition, and it is hoped that one day she will steam again. Her masts were removed a few years later (inset).

Maid of the Loch is now a 'designated vessel' on the UK's heritage list reflecting her importance as the last Clyde-built paddle steamer. That status makes access to funding sources a little easier. Her compound diagonal steam engines, currently being restored, were built by Rankin & Blackmore of Greenock, and their 900hp gave her a stop speed of 13.75 knots - 25.5mph. She was originally fitted with a Navy type boiler supplying a maximum pressure of 120lbs but that was removed and scrapped in 1996. She had two 10kW dc power generators and had a maximum bunker capacity of 17.5 tons of heavy fuel oil.

this period, ocean-going steamers were getting ever larger, although relatively small even by the standards of today's cross-channel ferries.

Brunel's revolutionary SS *Great Britain* was launched in Bristol in 1843 and first crossed the Atlantic under steam alone in the summer of 1845.

The world's first iron-hulled and propeller-driven passenger liner – twice the size of anything else afloat at the time of her launch – proved an expensive vessel to build. She was considered too heavy for available slipways, so was constructed in a specially-built dry dock – the one she is preserved in today.

On her maiden voyage from Bristol, sailing from London to Plymouth, and then on to Liverpool via Dublin, she averaged 11 knots. The first Atlantic crossing by a screw-driven ship began from Liverpool at 3.20pm on 26 July 1845, and ended off Governor's Island, New York, at 2.15pm on 10 August. She had travelled 3,304 miles at an average speed of just over 9 knots. She was designed to accommodate 360 passengers but only 45 braved that first crossing.

That first transatlantic crossing of the 3,000 ton vessel had taken a little

This Edwardian post-card of Trossachs Pier shows the steamer *Sir Walter Scott* shortly after she was introduced on to Loch Katrine. Behind her, moored and out of service, is her predecessor *Rob Roy*, which had spent 45 years sailing between Trossachs Pier and Stronachlachar. *Sir Walter Scott* has now served for more than 110 years.

The steamer *Sir Walter Scott*, seen here departing from Trossachs Pier in 2009, was launched on the Clyde in 1899, dismantled, moved in pieces to Stronachlachar on Loch Katrine, rebuilt, relaunched in 1900, and in service ever since! She has been remodeled and refurbished so many times that externally she is very different in appearance to her 1899 profile, but her engines are still those installed more than110 years ago by Denny Brothers. The 3-cylinder triple-expansion engine is powered by two locomotive boilers and drives a single screw, but the recent conversion to bio-fuel has robbed her of the plumes of smoke which used to trail behind her immediately after stoking.

less than fifteen days – a long time by today's standards, but she had achieved something which, in the 1840s, had been thought by many to be impossible.

In her 1843 configuration, SS *Great Britain* had a massive boiler, 34ft long, 31ft wide and just under 22ft high. It was sub-divided into three compartments, each of which could be isolated and shut down as required. The boiler – which delivered a maximum steam pressure of 5psi – was heated by

24 furnaces, 12 each end, with a total grate area of 1248sq.ft. The stokers who fed them each shoveled at least a ton of coal in their four-hour shift.

Walter Channing, a passenger on board in 1856, wrote of the conditions "The temperature in which these men work and live, when on duty, is 120 degrees Farenheit. When his short watch of two to four hours is over, the stoker comes upon deck, reeking of sweat".

SS *Great Britain* was not the first steamer to cross the Atlantic. That honour probably goes to the American paddle-steamer *Savannah* in 1819, which took 23 days for the crossing – but she had used her sails for part of the voyage.

The SS *Sirius* claimed the first crossing by steam alone as early as 1838 but, running out of coal, her crew reportedly burned furniture to complete the voyage! Brunel's paddler SS *Great Western* also completed her first crossing in 1838, but having been designed for transatlantic work, she had enough coal on board – so the furniture was safe!

Of all these pioneering vessels, only the SS *Great Britain* has been preserved, and the survival of this remarkable vessel – quite rightly recognised and feted as the first 'modern' liner – has come about by largely by default rather than design.

The earliest photo-graph of the SS *Great Britain* is believed to have taken by pioneer photographer William Henry Fox Talbot - who lived just a few miles away at Lacock Abbey in Wiltshire - while the ship was being fitted out in Bristol's Cumberland Basin in 1844. *(courtesy ss Great Britain Trust)*

The recreation of SS *Great Britain's* boiler room. The figures of the stokers were modelled on a group of Rolls Royce apprentices.

She may have been innovative in many ways, but she did not prove to be a viable financial proposition for her operators. She was eventually sold and extensively remodelled by her new owners. With more powerful engines – and with an additional funnel and two fewer masts – and a passenger capacity increased to over 700, in 1852 she began a regular service to Australia. Further modifications gave her one funnel again, and three square-rigged masts, but by 1876 her days as a passenger ship came to an end and she was laid up at Birkenhead for six years.

Under new owners again, her engines were removed, and she spent the remaining 4 years of her working life as a sailing ship, before disaster caused her to be abandoned in the Falklands.

There she lay for over fifty years, being used as a floating store until finally grounded and abandoned in Sparrow Cove in 1937. She lay there for 33 years until raised on to a floating pontoon in 1970 for the 7,000 mile voyage back home to Bristol.

Removed from the pontoon in Avonmouth on 5 July 1970 – afloat for the first time in 33 years and for the last time – she was towed up-river, under Brunel's Clifton Suspension Bridge back to the drydock which had been built especially for her construction.

That combination of ship and dock makes her a unique part of maritime history, and for 35 years, work progressed

Opposite: The replica engine installed into SS *Great Britain* in 2005 is a remarkable recreation of Thomas Guppy's 1000 hp 4-cylinder 1843 power plant. Guppy's engine was based on a design by Isambard Kingdom Brunel's father Marc, and was an engineering sensation at the time. The engine, which drove the propellor shaft via a massive chain drive, was so large it stood higher than the deck level. Originally *Great Britain* was designed to be driven by two paddle-wheels, so the orientation of the engine had to be turned by 90° when Brunel persuaded the Great Western Steamship Company that a propellor would give the ship much greater stability and ease of steering in the heavy seas she would experience in the North Atlantic

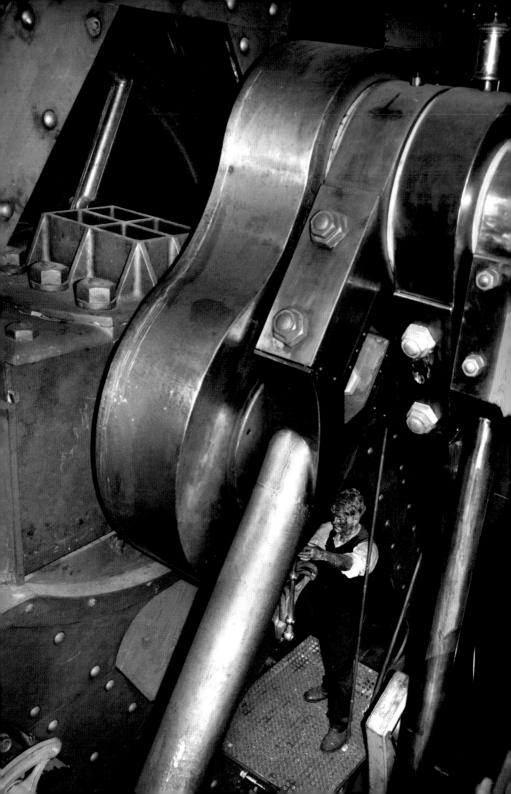

Left: When steamers like the SS *Great Britain* were operating under sail, the inactive propellor caused drag, slowing the vessel down. To avoid this, a 'propellor lift' was used which disengaged it from the drive shaft and raised the blades clear of the water.

Below: The replica propeller fitted to SS *Great Britain* in the early 1990s. The design proved remarkably efficient.

Opposite: For the biggest ship in the world, Guppy and Brunel built the biggest engine. Seen from above, the life-size figure of the engineer far below gives a real sense of its scale.

on returning her to her 1843 appearance. By 2005, the restoration project was complete, and the challenge now is preservation for the future.

Quite a number of later vessels have survived in conditions ranging from very poor and causing concern, to well preserved with their futures assured.

In Portsmouth's Royal Naval Dockyard since her restoration was completed in 1987, HMS *Warrior*, dating from 1860, is a fine example of an early iron-clad steam-powered

Britain's oldest-surviving steam-powered warship, the magnificently restored HMS *Warrior*, was built in 1860, entered service in 1861, but ended her working life ignominiously converted into Oil Fuel Hulk C77 in Pembroke Dock. Restoration took 7 years and £9M, and she returned to Portsmouth in 1987.

As an insurance policy, SS *Great Britain* carried 15,000sq.ft. of sail on six masts in addition to her steam engines. However, she crossed the Atlantic for the first time in 1845 without ever setting her sails.

warship. She is also an impressive yardstick as to how much steamship design had progressed in a little over a decade and a half. But, like SS *Great Britain*, much of what we see of HMS *Warrior* today is a reconstruction rather than a restoration. Her 50 years as a static fuelling hulk at Pembroke Dock in Milford Haven meant that little apart from her hull survives from her original configuration. Today what we see is as close as the restorers can get to her appearance – inside and out – as she entered service on 1 August 1861, the largest, fastest, heaviest and most modern warship in the world. Her radical design amazed all who saw her.

When SS *Great Britain* was launched she was the largest ship in the world. *Warrior* was launched 16 years later, and at 9,210 tons with a top speed of 14.5 knots under steam, she was nearly three times the weight, and half as fast again as Brunel's ship. *Warrior* is 100 feet longer than *Great Britain*, and a few feet wider. But even she was small by the standards of the day. Brunel had completed the *Great Eastern* in 1859, and she had a displacement of over 32,000 tons!

Although she was still a fully-rigged sailing ship, HMS *Warrior*'s powerful steam engines were more than capable of powering her along without wind assistance. The advantage, though, was relatively slight given the expense and hard work involved.

Each of her ten boilers was heated by four furnaces which had to be constantly fed with fuel by stokers working in temperatures which exceeded 50°C!

A large number of her 700-man crew were involved below decks, just keeping the fires burning and the steam engines working! For all their work, and the cost of the coal she burned, *Warrior* was only 1.5 knots faster under steam than she was under full sail!

The logistics and sums of money involved in preserving large vessels are staggering. HMS *Warrior* took two years to build, at a cost of just under £400,000. She took eight years to restore and rebuilt, at a cost said to be around £8M! In Bristol, the SS *Great Britain* restoration project took 35 years and many millions more!

The most famous surviving paddle steamer of them all, PS *Waverley* still regularly sails the Clyde and the Bristol Channel. Described as the 'world's last sea-going paddle steamer', she was built by A & J Inglis for the Caledonian Steam Packet Company. Sold for £1 in 1974 to ensure her preservation, some sources even claim Caldonian MacBrayne had to lend the preservation society the £1 to pay for her! The last paddle steamer to sail in CalMac's colours, in preservation *Waverley* sports the distinctive red white and black funnels of the LNER rather than either the buff and black of the CSPCo or the red and black of CalMac. Her home berth is now on the Clyde adjacent to Glasgow's futuristic new Science Centre.

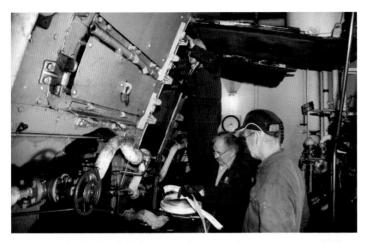

Opposite: The beautiful polished brass and wood wheel, telemotor and binnacle on the bridge of the SS *Shieldhall*, the only surviving operational twin-screw steamship in Europe. Using simple hydraulics, the telemotor sent the bridge commands to steering engine, back aft.

This page top: Replacing the firebox seals in *Shieldhall's* engine room. The two Scotch boilers are original, dating from the ship's construction in 1955. Formerly, asbestos would have been used to seal the firebox doors. Despite having fire-boxes and ash pans, *Shieldhall* has always been an oil-burner.

Middle: Detail of one of the ship's two 800ihp triple-expansion steam engines. The 1,792grt *Shieldhall* was designed as a sludge ship, and built in the Lobnitz yard in Renfrew.

Bottom: Servicing the steam pump – one of the ship's 22 steam engines – and its Stevenson's link valve gear, which injects fuel into the fire-boxes. Despite her size, *Shieldhall* is entirely maintained and crewed by volunteers.

Plans to preserve the 41,900 ton 1959-built P&O steam-turbine liner *Oriana* in the fast-growing city of Dalian in north-eastern China proved unrealistic. Seen here in January 2005, partially submerged after fire and storm damage the previous winter, she was destined to be broken up just weeks later.

And yet, around Britain, other massive restoration and rebuilding projects are underway at huge expense, preserving the last surviving examples of historically important ships. The National Historic Ships Collection includes several steam-powered vessels whose roles in British history are just too important to allow them to rot away or be broken up. Listings of the preserved ships – sail, steam and diesel – can be found at *www.nationalhistoricships.org.uk*

Amongst them are some relatively small wooden-hulled vessels whose preservation will place relatively manageable demands on their owners. Others are of such a massive scale that their long-term preservation will demand continuing large sums of money.

Current thinking is about the preservation of original fabric rather than its replacement. Iron hulls, especially once they are out of the water, are under constant attack from the elements, as can be seen in the significant corrosion of the hull of SS *Great Britain* since her return from the Falklands.

Fortunately the science of preservation is developing rapidly, and innovative, if expensive, solutions are being found to limit further erosion, and secure the future of these vessels. But, as is evidenced by some of the steamships which lie rusting at their moorings, good intentions are not enough – they need to be supported by on-going source of funds if preservation is going to do more than just delay the inevitable.

Opposite: Preserving and maintaining historic steamships is an enormously expensive under-taking, and very few attempts to do so have so far proved economically viable. The best laid plans sometimes eventually lead to no more than rusting and unsightly hulks, as can be seen in the gazetteer section of this book.

The 4,450 ton 1955 turbine steamer TSS *Duke of Lancaster* lies rusting away embedded in sand on the banks of the River Dee in North Wales. Plans to turn her into a leisure centre and nightclub failed.

Now permanently moored in Leith docks, HMY *Britannia's* future should be safe. The iconic 1953 turbine steam yacht may have lost her elegant lines due to the construction of a hideous visitor centre on her aft deck, but if ticket sales remain at their present level, she should continue to be commercially viable for the foreseeable future.

An industrial tank engine lies rusting in a siding in the early 1970s. Bringing locomotives like this back to life is a real labour of love – requiring good engineering skills, lots of patience, and a great deal of money.

INDUSTRIAL WORKHORSES

The practice of referring to steam locomotives as 'iron horses', so beloved of American cowboy movies, is an appropriate one, and nowhere more so than on the hundreds of industrial, mineral and colliery railways which already existed in Britain in the early 19th century. The advent of the steam engine displaced tens of thousands of horses, and many of the thousands of men who kept and worked them. Those who remained in employment had to adapt to new ways of working and acquire a whole new range of skills.

There was still plenty of work for blacksmiths, but instead of stablehands and cart-men, the steam work-horse required drivers, engineers and firemen. New jobs were created in coal mines, docks and harbours, and large factory complexes as steam engines became more and more commonplace.

Opposite: 0-6-0T *Lindsay*, completed in 1887, is the only surviving example of a locomotive built by the Wigan Coal & Iron Company. She was built to work the Standish Collieries, owned by the Earl of Crawford and Balcarres. 'Lindsay' was the Earl's family name. This photograph was taken on the occasion of her centenary in 1987. She is currently in store.

Opposite: 0-6-0ST No. 47, built in 1955 by Robert Stephenson & Hawthorns at their Newcastle works, and now known as *Moorbarrow*, is seen here about to run round the train at Mendip Vale on the East Somerset Railway in 2011. The locomotive was formerly operated by the Northumbrian Area of the National Coal Board.

Left: *Bellerophon* was built at Haydock Foundry in 1874 for use in the nearby Haydock Collieries in the south Lancashire coalfield. She is seen here at Crewe Heritage Centre in the late 1980s.

While steam was withdrawn from British Railways metals in the late 1960s, industrial steam remained in widespread use for more than a decade longer. Indeed, narrow gauge industrial engines were still being ordered and built in the 1970s. They are even making something of a return today.

Ex-NCB Scottish North Area Frances Colliery No.30 is now part of a static display adjacent to the preserved concrete colliery headgear in Lochore Meadows Country Park in Fife. Built by Barclay in 1949 with Works No.2259, the locomotive and headgear are now all that remain of once-extensive colliery workings and yards.

Two Hunslet engines stand at Embsay Station, on the Embsay & Bolton Abbey Railway in the early 1980s. No.69 was built in 1953 for use at the NCB's South Hetton Colliery in County Durham. It was withdrawn from service in 1984 for a major overhaul.

Opposite: 1953-built Hunslet 0-6-0ST *Cumbria* was acquired by the L&HR in 1973, since when the locomotive clocked up more than 100,000 miles on the heritage line's 3.5 mile track, the first former industrial locomotive to achieve such a feat.

Saddle tanks remained the major motive power source in many British collieries throughout most of the 1970s. Many of them were old, and rather tired and sad-looking, but they still performed the tasks for which they had been designed. There was little nostalgia towards them. Indeed stopping on a bridge over a colliery railway to watch a couple of Hunslets working hard to pull a enormous coal train was a spectacle appreciated by relatively few! Then, almost overnight, they were gone, replaced by small diesels which took a second rather than three hours to power up, much to the delight of those who worked them!

Industrial tank engines came in all shapes and sizes. They were small, powerful, locomotives, able to haul considerable loads of coal, iron, stone or whatever other commodity their owners were engaged in extracting or manufacturing.

They were also relatively fuel-efficient, and over the last forty years, they have proved to be ideal for use pulling an average of four or five coaches on the growing number of preserved steam railways throughout the country.

1953-built ex-War Department Hunslet 0-6-0ST *Errol Lonsdale* taking on coal at Buckfastleigh on the South Devon Railway. Since this photograph was taken, the locomotive has been sold to Belgium.

Below: Bagnall 0-6-0ST *Victor* prepares to pull a train away from Washford Station on the West Somerset Railway in 1986. Built in 1950 for use at Austin's Longbridge car plant, the locomotive is currently under restoration at the Lakeside & Haverthwaite Railway in Cumbria.

Opposite top: Hunslet 0-6-0ST *Repulse*, seen here about to leave Haverthwaite station, was constructed in 1950 for the National Coal Board and worked at the Ladysmith Washery in Whitehaven until withdrawn from service in 1974. Completely rebuilt, and with vacuum brakes fitted, she is now at the L&HR.

Opposite bottom: Ex-Manchester Ship Canal Company locomotive No.32, *Gothenburg*, taking on water at Bury during a tour of duty on the East Lancashire Railway.

While it may well be that it is the large mainline express engines which epitomise the success of the preservation movement and attract photographers whenever and wherever they are in steam, it is the small 0-4-0 and 0-6-0 tanks engines built by the likes of Andrew Barclay, Hunslet, Bagnall and Hudswell Clarke and others which actually do the lion's share of the day-today work on the heritage lines.

Industrial engines were built to work hard, and built to last. By the time industrial steam was being phased out, it was not unheard of for locomotive 70, 80 and more years old, to

still be performing the function for which they had been purchased.

Some historic names live on – The Hunslet Engine Company was founded as long ago as 1864, and has been associated with locomotive manufacture since the early days of steam. Their output was worldwide, and within a couple of years of being established, Hunslet had already shipped ten engines to Java, Indonesia. There is a pleasing symmetry to the knowledge that over 100 years later, the last of their output of over 2200 steam locomotives was also supplied to Java! For a long time, this was claimed to be the last British-built industrial steam locomotive. But now, 35 years after ceasing production, Hunslet is once again manufacturing

steam engines albeit for use on narrow-gauge lines rather than standard gauge!

At the time of writing, a 24" gauge Hunslet Quarry Class 0-4-0 saddle tank ready to run would set you back just £130,000 + VAT. Narrow gauge steam engines made up a significant proportion of those manufactured in Britain, and were widely used in quarries, docks and harbours, and other locations where access to mainline rolling stock was not required. While it may be standard gauge which draws the most attention, there are groups across the country working to keep the heritage of narrow gauge industrial steam alive and well.

At the height of industrial steam, many collieries had their own locomotive workshops, which handled much more than just day-to-day repairs of the engines and rolling stock.

Some even developed more extensive facilities, and built their own locomotives 'in-house' to unique and local designs, finely matched to the tasks in hand.

The Wigan Coal & Iron Company was just such an organisation, and their output of steam engines is now represented by a single survivor – *Lindsay*, an 0-6-0 saddle tank dating from 1887. Wigan C&I Co was an early example of integrated manufacturing, production and operation. The company made the iron and steel, manufactured the locomotives, and owned the extensive collieries and coal yards in which they were operated.

Colliery engines did not normally need to have large coal bunkers. There was enough of the stuff lying around the pit yard. When they needed stoking, they were briefly stopped while the crew picked coal up off the ground. Similarly, locomotives working in factory yards or docks rarely travelled more than a mile or two, so the ability to carry a lot of fuel would have been an unnecessary additional burden, reducing the load-hauling ability of the engine itself.

Opposite top: Detail of the running gear on a small Barclay tank seen on a Lancashire siding in 1975.

Opposite bottom: In the 1980s, coaches carrying assorted liveries were the order of the day. Here driver Tim Owen and fireman Tony Fell put on a show for the camera as Barclay 0-4-0ST *David* emerges from the tunnel on the Lakeside & Haverthwaite Railway 25 years ago. No. 2333 was built in Kilmarnock by Andrew Barclay Sons & Company for use at the Millom Ironworks in Cumberland, and entered sevice in January 1953. The locomotive returned to Cumbria when she was acquired by the Lakeside & Haverthwaite Railway in March 1978, and is still steamed regularly.

An 0-4-0 saddle tank at work at Bamfurling colliery near Wigan, photographed by Thomas Taylor in the 1880s. This unusual locomotive was built by Neilson of Glasgow.

NCB No.21 from the West Ayr Area is now a static exhibit in the Scottish Mining Museum at Lady Victoria Colliery in Newtongrange, Lothians. The 0-4-0 tank engine was manufactured by Andrew Barclay in Kilmarnock in 1949 with Works No.2284.

In steam on the Swindon & Cricklade Railway in 2009 after a seven year restoration, *Salmon*, Works No.2139, was delivered by Barclay in 1942 to Stanton Ironworks' Harlaxton Ironstone Quarries.

For use in some smaller factory yards, it even proved to be much more efficient to develop lightweight fireless locomotives which were periodically charged with pressurised steam produced in a static on-site boilerhouse. These, however, have limited application – or even appeal – on

today's heritage lines, so it is left to the Barclays, the Bagnalls, the Hunslets and others to keep the lines running.

Some of them have already covered several times as many miles in preservation as they ever did in the collieries, docks and industrial complexes for which they were originally commissioned.

Today, a remarkable total of more than 150 Barclay tank engines are known to still survive across the world in various states of repair and preservation, 135 of them in the UK, some as static exhibits, but many restored and operational. Outside the UK, there are six in South Africa, five in Australia, two in Spain, and one each in Argentina, India, Ireland and the USA. The number of surviving Hunslet-built locomotives is unknown, but believed to be of a similar order.

The industrial tank engine, cheap to run, and more than capable of pulling the normal length of a heritage line train, really is the daily workhorse of preserved steam lines.

Without them, the economics of running a short length of steam line in the 21st century, even relying on a volunteer workforce, would be quite impossible to justify.

NCB Ayrshire Region No.24, 1953-built Barclay 0-6-0 tank engine, Works No. 2235, awaits restoration in the yard of the Bo'ness & Kinneil Railway in the 1970s.

Above: The driver
of Pacific Class 7
No.70000 *Britannia*
waits for the signal
before pulling away
from the platform at
Carnforth. Built at
Crewe in 1951 as the
first of the Standard
Class 7 locomotives,
she is currently
back at Crewe
undergoing extensive
restoration.

MAINLINE STEAM

It was all supposed to end, neatly and tidily, on Saturday 3rd August 1968 when the 9.25pm Liverpool train left Preston Station, hauled by former LMS Stanier 'Black 5' No.45318, and crewed by driver Ernie Heyes and fireman Tony Smith. Thirty-five minutes earlier, the 8.50pm to Blackpool had left the same station hauled by 'Black 5' No.45212. These were the last scheduled steam-hauled passenger services to run on British Railways tracks. Several trains – which would become known as the 15 guinea specials – ran on the following day, 4 August, but after they had gone, it was firmly believed that steam locomotives would never again pull passenger trains on BR metals. The brave new world which had consigned many almost-new steam engines to the scrapheap envisaged a railway network which would become the exclusive domain of diesel and electric trains.

The British Railways Board had immediate plans to dispose of hundreds of engines, regardless of their age and condition – some were notably only eight years old – and all were scheduled for the cutter's torch. There was to be no turning back! Even 45212 and 45318 were to be discarded, with not a drop of sentiment shown towards the engines which had pulled

Main picture: LMS Jubilee Class 5593 *Kohlapur* emerges from clouds of steam during a steam cavalcade at Bury on the East Lancashire Railway in the early 1990s. *Kohlapur*, a three-cylinder Stanier-designed pacific, was built in Glasgow in 1934 by the North British Locomotive Company. In 1995 she was repainted in BR green, in which livery she remains despite plans to return her to LMS crimson lake.

Once a familiar
site across Britain,
coaling towers are
now relatively rare
reminders of the
age of steam. These
examples are at
Carnforth in
Lancashire. Plumes
of steam from
No.70000, *Britannia*,
preparing to pull a
train along the short
length of track which
was all that was
available in the days
of 'Steamtown', add
a nostalgic touch.

The drive gear of a
British Railways
Standard Class 4MT
2-6-4T tank engine.
Designed at British
Railways' Brighton
works in 1950, 155
examples of the
class were produced
between 1951 and
1956 - designed to
have a working life
of forty years!
The design was a
modification of
Fairburn's successful
design for a large
tank engine for the
LMS, and all but 25
of them were turned
out from Brighton.
Nos.80000-80009,
and 80054-80058
were constructed at
Derby, while 80106-
80115 were built at
Doncaster. 80135,
seen here, was
completed at
Brighton in 1956, and
is now preserved on
the North Yorkshire
Moors Railway.

those historic 'last scheduled steam passenger trains'. Sentiment about steam was unheard of in 1968.

But 45212 got a last minute reprieve. Built for the LMS by Armstrong Whitworth in Newcastle in 1935, she was to be disposed of as just another heap of unwanted metal. The day after her historic last journey, and with her boiler still warm from pilot duties at Preston station, she was bought by Yorkshire's newly-established Keighley & Worth Valley Railway. The age of the heritage railway had dawned, and 45212 was one of the first beneficiaries. For 45318, the story was very different. She was not one of the eighteen Black 5s to be rescued and preserved and met the same unceremonious end as hundreds of others.

And the '15 guinea specials' which were to bring down steam's final curtain? Well on 4 August 2008, they held a 40th anniversary re-run of several of those 'last' journeys.

In the intervening forty years, photographers have gathered on bridges and tracksides the length and breadth of the country to watch and photograph the mighty survivors as they steam past.

Black 5s, 45212 and 5025, stand ready for their day's work at Howarth sheds on the Keighley & Worth Valley Railway in 1975. 45212 was built at Armstrong Whitworth at Elswick, Newcastle, in present-day Merseyside in 1934. Between 1936 and 1951, a total of 832 Black 5s were constructed.

The last remaining steam engines had barely arrived at scrapyards all around the country when the preservation movement notched up a gear. Long before the fires were dropped from 45212 and 45318 on 4 August 1968, a limited future for standard gauge steam was already in place.

Ambitious plans had already been drawn up to marry branch lines – many of them closed by Beeching – with some of the many steam locomotives still in working condition, and recreate the magic of steam railways. And there were many miles to choose from – over 1000 miles of track had been closed in 1964, 600 more in '65, 750 in '66, 300 in '67 and a further 400 in 1968.

Indeed some heritage railway companies were effectively already in existence before the last steam service ran on British Railways.

Up in Cumbria, the Lakeside Railway Estates Company had been formed in 1966 with a view to preserving and reopening the former Furness Railway branch line to Lakeside on Windermere which had closed to passengers in the previous year. Out of that grew today's Lakeside & Haverthwaite Railway.

But the L&HR is a mere baby compared with the Bluebell Line in Sussex which in 2009 celebrated fifty years of preserved standard gauge steam. That is fifty years since the setting up of the Bluebell Railway Preservation Society, marking it as not only the first standard gauge steam railway preservation project in Britain, but in the world! However that

Opposite: Southern Railway 'Light Pacific' West Country Class locomotive *Bodmin* was completed at Eastleigh in late 1945 and given the SR number 21C116. Three years later she became 34016 under British Railways numbering. Originally completed with the same boxy outer casing used on other Bulleid West Country locomotives, *Bodmin* was rebuilt by British Railways in 1956 giving her a more conventional appearance. Withdrawn in June 1964 after having run over 800,000 miles, she was destined for the scrapyard. Rescued in 1971 and moved to Quainton in Buckinghamshire, she is seen here in 1973 part-way through her first major restoration. The locomotive was moved from Quainton to the Mid-Hants Railway in 1976, and returned to steam three years later.

The number '6229' identifies this rod assembly as belonging to LMS Stanier Pacific *Duchess of Hamilton*.

55

is nearly a decade younger than the world's oldest heritage line – the narrow-gauge Talyllyn Railway in Wales, which has been run by volunteers now for sixty years!

Steam engines which lay rusting away in scrapyards at Barry, Carnforth and elsewhere have been painstakingly restored and brought back into steam. Their age, however, is against them and ensuring their continued operation is increasingly costly.

45596 *Bahamas* approaching Wigan Wallgate station in the 1990s at the head of a heritage special. A total of 191 Jubilees were built between 1934 and 1936, at Crewe, Derby and Glasgow, and four have been preserved - *Bahamas*, *Kohlapur, Leander* (opposite) and *Galatea*, although *Galatea* is as yet in the early stages of restoration.

Leander, in LMS livery, photographed in the yards at Bridgenorth in the early 1990s.

Below: The cab of Black 5 No.4767 photographed at Steamtown, Carnforth, in the early 1970s. Now restored as 44767, and named *George Stephenson*, the locomotive was unique amongst the 842 Black 5s in having outside Stephenson link motion. After a major refit, 44767 returned to service in 2010 and currently splits its time between the North Yorkshire Moors Railway and the Churnet Valley.

Several new-builds are in various stages of construction. The first of them, Peppercorn A1 Pacific No.60163 *Tornado*, first moved under its own power in 2008, and attracts huge crowds wherever it goes.

The G5 Locomotive Company Ltd is currently building a new North Eastern Railway's Wordsell G5 0-4-4 tank engine from scratch at Great Northern Steam's Darlington Works – where the

The crew of the replica *Rocket* await the signal to set off as part of the cavalcade of steam during the celebrations in May 1980 to mark the 150th anniversary of the 1829 Rainhill Trials.

The two-cylinder *Locomotion No.1* was built by Robert Stephenson and Company in 1825, and it hauled the first train on the Stockton and Darlington Railway on 27 September that year. Withdrawn from service in 1841, the original is now preserved in the Darlington Railway Museum, as part of the National Collection. The nameplate illustrated here is on Beamish Museum's working replica, created in 1975 to mark the locomotive's 150th anniversary.

new A1 Tornado was completed just a few years ago, and only a short walk from the NER's North Road Shops where the original G5s were built more than a century ago. 110 of them were built at the company's North Road Works in Darlington between 1894 and 1901, but none survived into preservation. The North Road site is now occupied in part by a Morrison's supermarket.

The replica *Sans Pareil*. The original locomotive was designed by Timothy Hackworth for the Rainhill Trials in 1829, but proved inefficient and very fuel-hungry. The two vertically mounted cylinders gave the engine a strange rocking motion, and it had the unfortunate habit of expelling a lot of unburned coke straight up through the flue! It was withdrawn during the competition after one of the cylinders cracked.

59

The new G5 will be operated on heritage lines when it is completed – which was originally intended to have been by 2010, but at the time of writing in 2012, completion is probably still some years away!

There are other groups – like the Severn Valley Railway-based 82045 Steam Locomotive Trust – dedicated to building new examples of other classes for which none exists in preservation. In the case of 82045, the project is to build a Riddles Class 3MT 2-6-2 tank engine.

But everything was very different more than 185 years ago when steam-powered transport was a largely untried novelty.

The first steam trains ran two decades before there was a viable photographic process, so our knowledge of the earliest locomotives is based on original drawings, and that fact that a few far-sighted people saw fit to preserve some of the key

By the time the last locomotives were rescued from scrapyards – more than 20 years after they were withdrawn – they were just badly rusted hulks.

0-4-2 *Lion* was built in 1838, one of two locomotives built for the Liverpool & Manchester Railway by Todd, Kitson & Laird of Hunslet, Leeds. By 1859 she had been sold to the Mersey Docks & Harbour Board as a stationery pumping engine. She is now a static exhibit in Liverpool Museum.

Opposite: Saved in 1975 from Barry scrapyard, ex-GWR 2-6-2T Prairie tank 4561 returned to steam on the West Somerset Railway in the late 1980s. The locomotive is currently awaiting a major overhaul.

locomotives themselves. So it was left to wordsmiths and artists to describe and illustrate the scenes at the opening of the Stockton and Darlington Railway. Acknowledged as the world's first passenger-carrying steam railway, the Stockton and Darlington was approved by a series of Acts of Parliament between 1819 and 1825, and carried its first fare-paying passengers on 27 September 1825. Huge crowds gathered to watch the first train depart – with several hundreds hoping to get on board.

Carrying passengers by railway was not new – the Mumbles Railway in South Wales had been doing that since 1807 – but travelling behind a steam engine was an entirely novel experience!

Robert Stephenson & Company built two locomotives for the inauguration of the new railway – *Locomotion No.1* is the one everybody remembers, but her sister locomotive *Hope* was also on duty that day. *Locomotion* had the honour of pulling the inaugural train, but steam traction was used on

Opposite: R.A.Riddles designed the BR Standard Class 4 tank in the early 1950s, and 155 of them were built. 80105 was built at Brighton. After several years of service on the Bo'ness & Kinneil Railway, her boiler certificate expired in 2010 and she is awaiting a major overhaul. 80105 is seen here leaving Bo'ness station in September 2009.

No.71000, 4-6-2 Pacific *Duke of Gloucester*, in steam. Built at BR's Crewe Works in 1954, No.71000 was the prototype of a new Riddles-designed 8P class, but was the only one ever built. 71000 was withdrawn from service in 1962 and eventually consigned to the scrapyard. By the time a group of enthusiasts sought to rescue the locomotive for restoration in 1974, what was left was in a poor state. Rebuilt by the 71000 Steam Locomotive Trust, *Duke of Gloucester* eventually returned to steam in 1987.

only a section of the 26-mile track. It took *Locomotion* a total of two hours to cover the 12-miles which had been allocated to steam, with hundreds of passengers sitting in open coal wagons for the journey. One specially constructed passenger 'coach' had been built for the event – described as looking like a garden shed on wheels – and given the imposing name of *The Experiment*. The dignitaries who sat 'indoors' were spared the showers of soot and sparks which were blasted out of *Locomotion*'s tall funnel!

Locomotion had only been operating for three years when the boiler exploded and killed the driver – the world's first railway fatality. Rebuilt, she continued in service until 1841, followed by 16 years as a stationary engine. In 1857, she was saved for preservation – so the world's oldest steam locomotive has, in fact, been in preservation for nearly ten times as long as she was operational on the rails!

When the Stockton & Darlington Railway's centenary was celebrated in July 1925, fifty-three locomotives took part in a major cavalcade – the first staging of an event with which we

BR Standard Class 4, 75069, seen here by the coal yard at Bridgenorth, was one of a class of 80 locomotives built at Swindon between 1951 and 1957, so some were little more than a decade old when scrapped. 6 have been preserved. Currently only 75029 on the NYMR is operational.

Just what we all turn up for – the crew of No.70000 *Britannia* make a splendid show for photographers as they prepare to pull a trainload of enthusiasts away from the platform. One of only two examples of the Britannia Class to survive from a build of 55, the locomotive is now privately owned and currently undergoing a major refit. The other, 70013 *Oliver Cromwell*, is part of the National Collection.

Bulleid 'West Country Class' 34092 *City of Wells* arrives in a cloud of steam at Oxenhope station on the Keighley & Worth Valley Railway in the 1990s. One of the first of the West Country Class engines to be completed after nationalisation, 34092 entered service in September 1949. The locomotive is currently undergoing a major rebuild.

Main picture: A busy day at Pickering station on the North Yorkshire Moors Railway in the 1990s. Thomson K1 Class 2-6-0 No.2005 prepares to pull a train away from the platform tender first. The locomotive was built at the North British Railway Works in Glasgow in 1949 – after nationalisation – for work on the Eastern Region of British Railways. Since this photograph was taken, it has been repainted in BR black and its BR number of 62005 has been restored.

inset far right: No.6960 prepares to leave Bridgenorth. Swindon-built in 1944, *Raveningham Hall* is one of six 'Modified Halls' in preservation, the others being 6984 *Owsden Hall* and 7903 *Foremarke Hall* at the Goucestershire Warwickshire Railway, 6989 *Wightwick Hall* at Quainton, and 6998 *Burton Agnes Hall*, a static exhibit at Didcot. A seventh, No.7927 *Willington Hall*, is currently in bits at Llangollen.

are today still very familiar. Amongst them, having already been in preservation for nearly seventy years, was *Locomotion No.1*.

Robert Stephenson had, by the time the Stockton & Darlington opened in 1825, moved on to a much bigger project – the proposed Liverpool & Manchester Railway, another of the key developments in the history of steam traction.

Deciding on the type of locomotive which would be best suited to the route led to the staging of the famous Rainhill Trials in October 1829 from which Stephenson's *Rocket* emerged triumphant. The Liverpool & Manchester opened in the following year, 1830, and its centenary was also celebrated by a cavalcade of steam power past and present.

May 1980 saw the anniversary celebrations of the Rainhill Trials bring together what was then the largest and widest selection of locomotives – from replicas of *Rocket* and *Sans*

Opposite top: More than 400 examples of John Aspinall's Class 27 0-6-0 locomotives were built between 1889 and 1899 for the Lancashire & Yorkshire Railway. A further 84 were completed under Henry Hoy and George Hughes. Here No.1207 and crew are photographed shortly after completion at the Horwich Locomotive Works in 1893. Note that the livery and crest are both much simpler than that normally carried by L&YR freight locomotives.

Opposite bottom: Three years later, No.1300 was completed. After the L&YR was absorbed into the LMS it was classed as '2F' and carried the LMS number 12322. Over 300 of the Aspinalls were still running when the LMS took over, and nearly 50 survived into the last years of BR steam but only this one, BR number 52322 was preserved. As LMS 12322, the locomotive is currently at the East Lancashire Railway.

Left: The sole survivor of LNER Class D49, 4-4-0 No.246 *Morayshire* reverses away from a siding at Bo'ness in 2010. She *was* built in Doncaster in 1928 and saved for preservation in 1962.

69

LNER A4 *Sir Nigel
Gresley* running light
through Rainhill
station in Merseyside
in 1980, during the
cavalcade marking
the 150th anniversary
of the Rainhill Trials
in 1829.

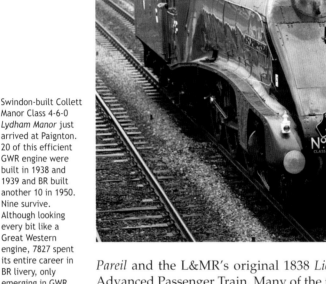
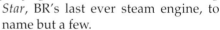

Swindon-built Collett
Manor Class 4-6-0
Lydham Manor just
arrived at Paignton.
20 of this efficient
GWR engine were
built in 1938 and
1939 and BR built
another 10 in 1950.
Nine survive.
Although looking
every bit like a
Great Western
engine, 7827 spent
its entire career in
BR livery, only
emerging in GWR
disguise after
preservation.

Pareil and the L&MR's original 1838 *Lion*, to BR's ill-fated Advanced Passenger Train. Many of the famous names were there – *Sir Nigel Gresley*, *Flying Scotsman* and 9F 2-10-0 *Evening Star*, BR's last ever steam engine, to name but a few.

Lion had been rescued from work as a pumping engine on Liverpool Docks, and restored to working order in time for the L&MR's centenary in 1930. She steamed again at Rainhill, and has appeared at many other cavalcades and commemorative events in the decades that followed, but due to her advancing frailty, has recently been retired and is now preserved as a static exhibit.

Lion's most onerous undertaking was undoubtedly the 1500 miles she

Recreating a branch line station platform at Beamish Open Air Museum Northumberland.

ran during her starring role in the 1952 Ealing comedy film *The Titfield Thunderbolt*.

With standard gauge heritage steam now established for more than half a century and still growing, some pundits believe heritage railways face a looming crisis – their locomotives are getting older, they are having to work harder, and maintenance costs are getting ever higher. New-builds may

Many heritage lines seek to recreate the romantic image of the branch line station, so vividly portrayed in this Edwardian postcard of Southwold station in Suffolk.

prove cheaper to operate, but will they have the same tourist draw as the great names from the past? Only time will tell. The pundits may be wrong, of course – for pundits in the 1960s believed steam would die out as soon as BR consigned their last locomotives to the breakers!

Given the age and multiple-ownership of many of the surviving locomotives, arguments rage over how they should be presented. *Flying Scotsman*, for example, was built for the Great Northern Railway, excelled under LNER ownership, and was fundamentally rebuilt during that time. Under British Railways ownership, further far-reaching modifications were made. For the National Railway Museum, which now owns the engine, and for the several previous owners since her withdrawal from mainline steam, how she is presented can never please everybody. As LNER 4472 and LNER 103, she was painted in apple green. As BR 60103 she was in lined black, with German smoke deflectors fitted. Her livery as 4472, in apple green and with smoke deflectors, was a combination of colour, number and profile which she never had when in service. Does that matter? It seems that it does matter to some purists! While she was undergoing a recent major rebuild, steam enthusiasts waited to see how she would be outshopped this time! The locomotive emerged briefly in the spring of 2011 painted in LNER wartime black, and carrying her two wartime numbers, one on each side of the cab. But by

Opposite: Caledonian Railway 419 running light after the last train of the day on the Bo'ness & Kinneil Railway, photographed in the late 1970s.

Insets: Scottish manufacturers' and operators' plates.

Below left: 0-6-0T 41708 prepares to depart from Swanage station for Corfe Castle on the Swanage Railway in Dorset. Built in Derby for the Midland Railway in 1880, the locomotive is now based at the Barrow Hill Railway Centre near Chesterfield in Derbyshire.

Below right: North Yorkshire Moors Railway's class 4MT 2-6-4 tank engine stands at the platform in Pickering station on a cold foggy morning.

the summer of 2011, she was, once again, in her familiar apple-green. During her rebuild – which took more than five years – the A4 boiler she had carried since the 1980s was replaced by the only surviving A3 boiler, bought as a spare when the locomotive was saved for the nation. Her old boiler is destined to be fitted into the Gresley A4 *Bittern*.

1937-built A4 Pacific *Sir Nigel Gresley*, rescued for preservation in 1966, spent many years of heritage service in LNER livery as No. 4498 – a livery she carried for only nine years in mainline service. From 1946 until nationalisation, *Gresley* carried the LNER number 7. Now, after a major rebuild by owners, The Sir Nigel Gresley Locomotive Preservation Trust Ltd, and operated by the A4 Locomotive Society Ltd, *Gresley* appears as BR 60007, painted in British Railways' post-war blue livery.

Over the years, A4s have appeared in no fewer than six different liveries. The first four locomotives were painted silver, the remaining 31 appearing in blues, greens and black over the years until they were decommissioned. Six of these magnificent locomotives survive; one each on static display in the USA – *Dwight D Eisenhower* – and Canada – *Dominion*

LMS's finest, 4-6-2 Princess Royal class 6201 *Princess Elizabeth* seen here at her operating base at Crewe Heritage Centre. As Works No.107, she was built at Crewe in 1933. From a class of thirteen locomotives. *Princess Elizabeth* and 6203 *Princess Margaret Rose* were the only two preserved.

of Canada. The remaining four – *Bittern, Mallard, Sir Nigel Gresley* and *Union of South Africa* are all in Britain.
Mallard is a static exhibit at the National Railway Museum, but the other three are operational. *Bittern* has recently assumed other identities, including *Silver Link*, and at the time of writing the locomotive is masquerading as *Dominion of New Zealand*.

Of the LMS classics, *Duchess of Hamilton* – also part of the National Collection – has been re-streamlined, regaining the profile she presented from 1938 until 1946 when it was removed to speed up maintenance. With her boiler certificate now expired, she is a static exhibit. Sister Princess Coronation Class locomotive 6233 *Duchess of Sutherland* remains operational. 6235 *City of Birmingham* is preserved as a static exhibit at Birmingham's 'Thinktank' museum.

As the cost of operating such large locomotives increases exponentially, we may see more and more of them limited to only a few main line runs.

In the decades of preservation, the patterns of operation on heritage lines have changed dramatically, with large locomotives largely limited to longer stretches of track.

4498 *Sir Nigel Gresley* stands outside Carnforth sheds in the mid 1990s after an overhaul and repaint. Now owned and operated by the Sir Nigel Gresley Locomotive Preservation Trust Ltd, and running under her BR number of 60007, Gresley was returned to steam in 2010 after a major rebuild.

BR 2-6-0 Standard Class 4 76079, now named *Trevor T. Jones*, stands in the yard at the East Lancashire Railway, Bury in the mid 1990s. Through the frames can be seen Stanier 8F 48431, the only surviving Swindon-built example of this heavy freight locomotive. Behind 76079 stands 53809, one of only two survivors of the 7F locomotives built between 1918 and 1925 for the S&DJR. 53809 returned to steam in 2006, and operates on the Midland Railway tracks at Butterley. The other example, No.88 and in S&DJR colours, is on the West Somerset Railway.

When the artist David Shepherd opened the East Somerset Railway in 1973, his large engines were regularly steamed. Seeing 9F 92203 *Black Prince* operate even over the short two miles of track was a great attraction.

Maintaining these large engines is getting harder, and more demanding on the wallets of their owners. *Black Prince* was out-shopped from Swindon in 1959, only a year before *Evening Star*, the last BR steam locomotive to be built, so she is now well over half a century old. David Shepherd himself, writing in the ESR's guidebook as long ago as 1996, drew attention to the escalating costs of maintaining his 9F "I know because of what I paid for *Black Prince* 29 years ago as I write (it is a sobering thought that I have owned her for almost four times her working life on British Rail), the major overhaul that she is undergoing at this time is costing over ten times what I paid for her, complete and in working order." A decade and a half later, those costs are several times higher.

Today, operating a locomotive the size of a 9F on a short line would be completely uneconomic – the cost of coal prohibitive – so trains on the East Somerset Railway are regularly hauled by small industrial engines, or GWR stalwart No.5637, a 1925-built Collett 56xx class 0-6-2 tank, and *Moorbarrow*, Robert Stephenson & Hawthorn's 1955-built 0-6-0ST.

But as the ESR was built as a branch-line – originally to Brunel's broad gauge – seeing trains hauled by tank engines rather than mainline locomotives has greater authenticity.

Black Prince, still owned by David Shepherd, is now steamed regularly on the Gloucestershire & Warwickshire Railway, and pays guest visits to other lines.

There are, thankfully, still a few enthusiasts with enough passion and deep enough pockets to keep these handsome and historic engines operational. The skills necessary to maintain them are also being passed on to the next generation through training programmes, and the facilities needed to overhaul them, and to manufacture new parts, are available at centres such as Pete Waterman's London & North Western Railway Heritage Company Limited at Crewe. Now employing more than fifty staff trained in the intricacies of steam locomotive maintenance, the company can undertake preservation and maintenance projects from the overhaul of complete locomotives to the manufacture of bespoke components. Without such facilities, more and more steam locomotives would just become museum exhibits.

Contrary to what the doctor ordered nearly half a century ago, the future for steam-powered railways in Britain seems remarkably bright. Let's hope it is also sustainable.

USA Transportation Corps S160, No.5820, built by the American Locomotive Company in 1942, was one of over 400 of the class to work British metals during the Second World War. Sold to Polish State Railways after the war, 5820 eventually returned to steam on the Keighley & Worth Valley Railway. Seen here in steam in the early 1990s, the locomotive now known as *Big Jim*, one of eight S160s preserved on British heritage lines, is currently nearing the end of a major overhaul.

LNER A3 Pacific No.4472, *Flying Scotsman* was built in 1923 at Doncaster for the Great Northern Railway

Below: Carrying British Railways No.46229, but painted in LMS Crimson Lake, 4-6-2 *Duchess of Hamilton* steams through Rainhill station in 1980. As LMS 6229, she was originally outshopped at Crewe in 1938, as one of the Princess Coronation Class of streamlined locomotives. Now streamlined once again *(inset)* and back in LMS livery, the Duchess is displayed as a static exhibit at the National Railway Museum in York.

THE NATIONAL RAILWAY COLLECTION

Given the country's pioneering role in the development of the railway, it took Britain a long time to establish a National Railway Collection, despite the idea having been talked about more than sixty years before it came into being. By the time the National Collection was established, many priceless examples of early railway vehicles had been broken up. The early locomotives and coaching stock which had survived had done so, in many cases, by accident rather than design.

Indeed, by the time the National Railway Museum was formally established in 1968, several key locomotives had already been bought privately to save them from destruction! Of all of those, 4472 *Flying Scotsman* eventually made it into the National Collection only in 2004.

Maunsell-designed 4-6-0 No.850, *Lord Nelson*, was built in 1926 at Eastleigh for the Southern Railway. Under BR it carried No.30850 until withdrawn in 1962. The only example to survive from a class of 16, the locomotive is now part of the National Collection, and is currently based at the Mid-Hants Railway. *Lord Nelson* has run regularly on the main line since preservation.

Edward Fletcher's
1875-built NER,
No.910 2-6-0 was
constructed at
Gateshead, and
originally preserved
as part of the NER's
collection long
before the National
Railway Museum.
Now displayed at
'Locomotion' at
Shildon. Beyond
No.910 is L&YR's
Horwich-built 2-4-2T
No.1008 from 1889,
works No.1, the first
of its class.

The interior of the
cab of the Great
Northern Railway's
G Class 4-2-2 'Stirling
Single' No.1, built in
1870 at Doncaster.
A total of 53 of the
class were built
between 1870 and
1895; the NRM's
example being the
only one to be
preserved. The
locomotive with its
distinctive 8ft 1in
driving wheels could
achieve a top speed
well over 80mph.
Despite its age, it
has been regularly
steamed over the
years, and is
currently on display
at the NRM's
Locomotion museum
at Shildon.

Several important locomotives had been saved and stored by the private railway companies over the years, but only the North Eastern Railway had made any serious attempt to establish a collection – and had chosen their storage facilities at York as the base. As long ago as the 1880s, the NER had started assembling key locomotives and rolling stock from its early days, although it would be a further 40 years – well into the LNER days – before a museum was opened at York.

Evening Star, Class 9F No.92220, only 20 years old when this photograph was taken, was the last steam locomotive built for British Railways, completed in 1960 and withdrawn from service only 5 years later. Evening Star has now been in preservation for nearly ten times as long as she was in mainline service.

Below: Class 5MT No.5000 was chosen as the NRM's example of the 842 'Black 5s' which were built. This example, in LMS lined black, was built at Crewe in 1938, and preserved because at the time it was closest to its original condition.

The LMS preserved a number of locomotives and some rolling stock – especially Royal Trains – at Euston, but by the 1930s was actually breaking up some of those stored. They did also offer a token engine to the LNER's museum, as did both the Southern and the Great Western, adding the London & North Western Railway's *Columbine* from 1845, the London Brighton & South Coast Railway's *Gladstone* from 1882, and Great Western's 1903 record-breaker *City of Truro* to the displays at York.

After nationalisation, ambitious plans were drawn up, not only to preserve key equipment, but also to open regional museums across Britain where preserved vehicles could be seen and enjoyed in the areas where they had worked. That never happened in

Above: Midland Railways 115 Class 4-2-2 locomotive No.673 in steam 1980.

Right: The National Railway Museum's main hall in the early 1970s. Nearest the camera is Wilson Worsdell's NER 4-4-0 No.1621, built at Gateshead in 1893. It was withdrawn in 1945. Beyond it is Wainwright-designed Class D1 4-4-0 No.737, built at Ashford Works in 1901 for the South Eastern & Chatham Railway and withdrawn from service in 1956. Beyond that is 46229 *Duchess of Hamilton*.

Hardwicke stands at the head of a rake of classic coaches, awaiting the signal to set off. Apart from the modern housing in the background, this scene could be from a century ago. The 2-4-0 Improved Precedent Class locomotive was designed by F. W. Webb. *Hardwicke* was built in Crewe in 1873, and is the only survivor of a batch of 166 for the London & North Western Railway. *Hardwicke* was withdrawn from service in 1932 and is now on static display at the NRM.

the intended manner, although locomotives and rolling stock, as well as assorted ephemera from the National Collection can be see at Swindon's 'Steam' Great Western Museum, the Glasgow Museum of Transport, and various other museums and heritage railways throughout the country. Other locomotives went for a time to the short-lived British Museum of Transport in Clapham – a site now graced by a large Sainsbury's supermarket!

One of Dr Beeching's lesser known decisions in the early 1960s was that British Railways should stop operating museums, so when the National Railway Museum was finally established in 1968, it was as a branch of the Science Museum and, based in York, it was to become the first national museum to be established outside of London.

The collection now runs to well over 100 steam locomotives out of a total of nearly 300 vehicles, hundreds of thousands of documents and other ephemera telling the story of Britain's railways.

About a third of the locomotives and vehicles are displayed at York at any given time, with many more at Shildon and in London's Science Museum.

Several are also to be found either working, or as static displays, on heritage lines, and those with mainline certificates and with appropriate safety and braking equipment added, can be seen as they were meant to be seen – at the head of summer specials, back running on the main line. That was something never envisaged or considered in *The Reshaping of British Railways*, Dr Richard Beeching's 1963 master plan.

ROAD AND FARM ENGINES

Each year the number of steam fairs in Britain seems to increase, as does the number of people drawn to them. There is something about the combination of a warm summer's day and the smell of the hot oil and coal smoke from steam engines which never fails to attract. You can smell it, often long before you can see it, so even waiting in queues to get into car parks is, for once, not an entirely unpleasant experience.

Some of the biggest and best of Britain's annual gatherings of steam engines have been established now for decades, but no matter where you live, you are probably not more than an hour from a steam fair at some time during the summer and autumn months. The shapes, the colours, the smell, and above all, the power of these magnificent machines makes them an enduring and growing attraction for all ages.

When Aveling & Porter of Rochester in Kent modified an early steam engine – which required to be horse-drawn to wherever its power was needed – into the first self-powered engine in the 1850s, they can never have foreseen the enduring impact their experiment was to have on rural Britain. Even less likely is that they could have foreseen that their design for an industrial workhorse would have become, more

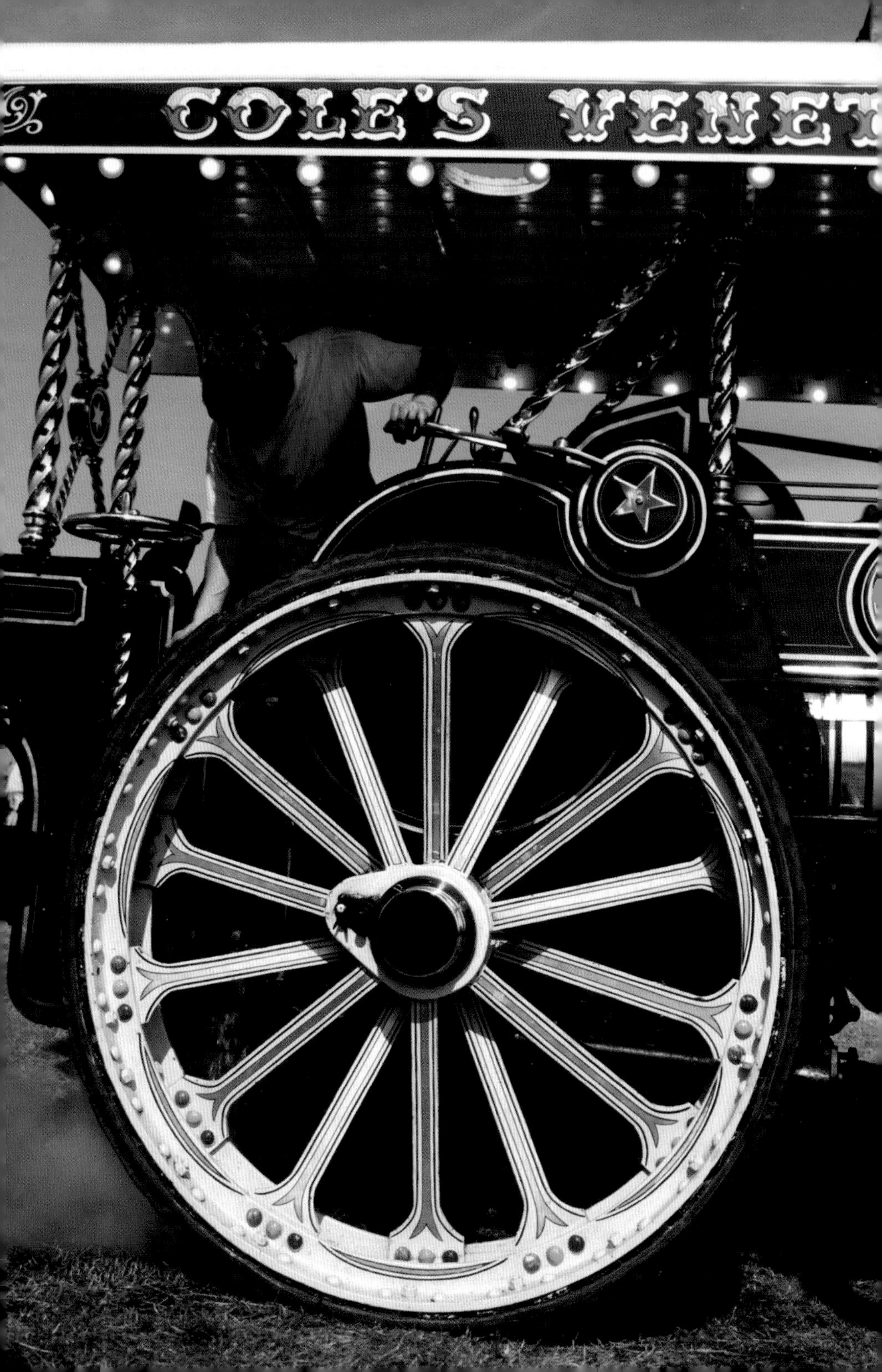
COLE'S

than a century and a half later, a magnet for tens of thousands of tourists across the British Isles.

These massive and powerful machines – some horse-drawn but the majority self-powered – were built in their tens of thousands over a period of a little more than a century, the first of them in the 1840s at the birth of the steam age.

The first of the self-powered engines rolled off the production line befoe 1860, and what is believed to have been the last – a steam-powered road-roller – left the Vickers Armstrong factory on Tyneside in 1950.

There were almost one hundred companies involved at one time or another in the construction of traction engines, road-rollers and steam powered cars and lorries but, despite that, the market was dominated by just a few well-known names. Amongst them are John Fowler & Sons of Leeds, Aveling & Porter of Rochester in Kent, Charles Burrell of Thetford, Norfolk, Richard Garrett of Leiston in Suffolk, and Joseph Foden of Sandbach in Cheshire – perhaps best known for steam powered lorries, and a name still proudly carried on the juggernauts which run up and down our motorways.

Just as would happen to the steam railway locomotive a few years later, when the decision was made to develop and promote the internal combustion engine for heavy haulage, steam road engines were abandoned and scrapped with an almost indecent haste.

Opposite: *Little Billy*, a 7.5 ton Garrett engines from 1919 - Works No.33566 - was originally built for Brownings of Stonehouse in Gloucester, and cost just over £1000 new. It was sold to W. Cole & Sons of Bristol in 1921 who converted it into a showman's engine. *Little Billy* spent nearly a quarter of a century powering Cole's Venetian Gondola ride - the ride itself is now preserved as part of the Thursford Collection in Norfolk. The beautifully restored engine is a popular attraction at steam fairs across the south-west.

Nottingham Goose Fair c.1906. A century ago most fairground rides were steam powered, although a few were electric.

Two decorated showman's engines steam past each other at the West of England Steam Engine Society's rally at Stithians near Truro.

Left: *Cornishman* was built by Garrett in Leiston, Suffolk, in 1912 carrying Works No.30959. It was supplied new to John Griffiths of Bargoed in Glamorgan but was later converted into a road-roller. It was returned to its original specification during restoration.

Below: Aveling & Porter engine Works No.9179, *Whippet* was originally outshopped from the company's factory in Rochester, Kent, in 1920. Some time thereafter it was converted into a showman's engine and assumed the appearance seen here. Within the last few years it was been restored to its original role as a general purpose engine, and repainted in deep red.

The Burrell Patent
Tractor, Works
No.3808, *Forrester*
built in 1919. Seen
here at a Cumbrian
steam rally in the
late 1970s, the
engine has since
been fully overhauled
and repainted in
green with red and
gold lining.

Burrell Tractor,
Works No.3862,
Little Dorothy was
built in 1921, and
in preservation has
carried the livery of
J. Johnson of Banks
and 'No.12' for over
forty years.

However, many hundreds escaped the cutter's torch – often by default rather than design – and lay for years abandoned in scrapyards. Thanks to the enthusiasm of collectors and restorers, many have been rebuilt.

There are, for example, almost 150 surviving examples of Aveling & Porter engines – the oldest being the Science Museum's Works No.721 from 1871, and the youngest being the privately owned *Ultimus* from 1937, which carried Works No.14187.

There are many hundreds of preserved Garretts, Fowlers, Burrells and others in total, and some treasured examples from the smaller and less well-known manufacturers. Together with other engines being progressively returned to steam, they promise the growing numbers of enthusiasts ever better experiences at steam fairs throughout the country.

Of course, the term 'traction engine' today embraces a wide range of industrial and agricultural steam engines, with a very wide range of functions. Steam was *the* source of power for so many years, and was applied to driving just about everything from the humble monolithic road roller to the delicate and tuneful fairground organ. And self-powered steam engines worked every sort of farmyard and field tool – ploughing,

Swinton Urban District Council's Aveling & Porter Invicta steam-roller, Works No.10915 was purchased new by the council in 1924.

Steam rollers line up ready to show off their power at a Lancashire vintage steam rally. Closest to the camera is the front roller of *Old Ernie*, a Burrell road-roller from 1913, Works No.3535, which was operated for many years by Leyland District Council in Lancashire. Beyond is *Friend Richard*, built by Wallis & Steevens in 1923 with Works No.7851. Over fifty examples of Wallis & Steevens engines have been preserved. This example is in Alan Atkinson's collection in Lancashire.

The front view of *Betsy*, the Invicta steam roller restored by the late Fred Dibnah. Built in 1910, with Works No.7632, it was purchased new by Flintshire County Council and sold for scrap in the 1960s.

harrowing, threshing, lifting, sawing, pumping and draining to name but a few. Demonstrations of steam ploughing, sawing and threshing are amongst the greatest crowd-pullers at fairs.

On the roads, huge steam engines pulled 'road trains' across Britain – only they had the power and endurance to draw heavy loads for long distances. And as Britain moved ever closer to WW1, the War Department purchased fleets of heavy engines to support Britain's armies in the field. The sheer size of some of these engines is awesome, and thankfully steam rallies and fairs still afford opportunities to get up close enough to appreciate the size.

In sharp contrast to the often-drab working garb of the farm and industrial engines, showman's engines were painted in bright colours and kept meticulously clean. They were admired as much in their heyday as they are today. They had two purposes. First they were the workhorses which hauled fairground rides and caravans around the country, and secondly, with their steam-driven generators, they were the power sources which lit the brightly-coloured fairground rides. Many engines were built especially for fairground use,

The well-worn front wheel of *Hero*, built by J & H McLaren & Co of Hunslett, Leeds, in 1918, Works No.1552. This 22 ton ploughing engine is believed to be the sole surviving example of its type. The drum of steel hawsers can be seen below the boiler. Some early examples of the company's tractors survive – dating back to the 1880s. By the end of the Great War McLarens were already developing petrol engines to supersede steamers, and the company started building machines powered by McLaren-Benz diesel engines in the 1920s. They continued to manufacture and supply heavy machinery into the 1950s. Since this photograph was taken, *Hero* has been fitted with thick rubber over-tyres to improve its handling on the roads.

The Britannia badge on the front of a 1920s Marshall road roller.

while others were converted from general purpose vehicles. And despite their outward appearance, beneath the glitter, paint and bright lights there were some very versatile and powerful vehicles indeed. They had to be – for during fairs they were working constantly keeping the showgrounds lit and alive, and when the fairs closed there was no respite as they hauled the dismantled rides to their next venue.

The typical full-length canopy over a showman's engine was partly for show, but more importantly it helped to keep the worst of the weather off the generating equipment.

The development of a design for an integral central steam engine in the middle of fairground carousels – believed to

A Fowler B6 Class heavy road engine, one of many built for the War Department in 1914, and later sold and converted for non-military use after the end of the Great War. Engines of this type this had first been used for hauling heavy military equipment in the 2nd Boer War in South Africa from 1899. When restored to steaming condition, this one was returned to its original military appearance and paintwork and given the name *Lafayette*.

Alan Atkinson's 1925 steam roller HO6459, *Friend Richard*, in steam. It was built by Wallis & Steevens of Basingstoke.

This Edwardian postcard of Fareham Creek near Portsmouth in Hampshire includes an Aveling & Porter steam roller, with caravan and trailer, parked near roadworks c.1904. Aveling & Porter produced their first steamroller as early as 1865.

have first been pioneered and patented by J. H. McLaren of Basingstoke in 1880 – may have eventually reduced the workload of the showman's engine while fairs were in operation, but increased the load which had to be hauled between venues.

The dedicated carousel engine was a dead weight which had to be loaded on to a trailer for transportation. Certainly

Fowler's 1920 *Bertha* worked as a showman's road engine until abandoned in 1943. After lying in a field for many years, the engine was purchased for restoration, changing hands several times before eventually steaming again in 1964. Regularly steamed throughout the 1960s '70s and '80s, *Bertha* can be seen in steam most weekends at Levens Hall, Cumbria.

Right: Fowler engine Works No.11111 *City of Hull* was built in 1910 and sold to the Hull Corporation. Rebuilt since this photograph was taken, the engine now has a canopy again.

the self-contained steam carousel seems to have been in widespread use by the Edwardian era, if the rides illustrated in contemporary postcards of fairs are typical.

Just as with steam railway locomotives, there are now societies dedicated to gathering and sharing knowledge on both major and minor manufacturers, and growing numbers of enthusiasts involved in restoring, maintaining and presenting these magnificent engines.

Increasingly detailed information on the growing lists of restored and operational engines is being gathered together

The maker's plate of Burrell road roller 3535, built in Thetford in 1913.

Left: The 1910-built, 10 Ton, slide valve, single cylinder, 4 Shaft, Aveling & Porter road roller *Betsy*, restored and owned by Bolton's legendary steeple-jack steam champion and television personality, the late Fred Dibnah. It is seen here on display at the East Lancashire Railway shortly before Fred's death in 2004. Named after his mother, it took Fred almost 25 years to rebuild the engine.

Steam-testing engines takes place every year before collections open at the start of each season. Here, the test steaming of the two engines which provide steam for many of the fairground rides at Hollycombe in Hampshire is underway. *Big John*, bottom left, a 12hp engine, was built in 1906 by Ruston Proctor to power farm machinery while *Bernadette*, bottom right, was built by Brouhot in 1896. *Eileen*, other pictures, was built as a traction engine by Clayton & Shuttleworth in 1917, intended for export to Russia, but later was converted to a straw-burning portable farm engine.

and published on specialist websites, and specialist magazines such as *Old Glory* and *Vintage Spirit*, dedicated to telling the stories of the engines and reporting on their public appearances, are growing in popularity.

The number of working engines of all shapes and sizes in Britain is probably approaching four figures – well over that if steam lorries and steam-powered cars are included in the lists – and still growing. They are smaller and therefore less expensive than railway locomotives to restore and maintain, and usefully much cheaper to operate.

Even the youngest surviving traction engines are now well over sixty years old, and it is a testament both to the craftsmanship of the original builders and to the skill of the restorers that so many of them are turned out in such splendid condition most summer weekends. There are many more still in the process of restoration.

Opposite: Burrell 1895 engine No.1876 Emperor *was delivered to George Twigdon & Sons of Dunton Bassett, Leicestershire. The oldest surviving showman's engine, it is also the only surviving single crank compound.*

Another view of showman's engine Bertha, *built by John Fowler & Co of Leeds. Fowlers were established in Hunslett, Leeds, as early as 1863.*

Opposite: The famous Foden badge has graced the front of many hundreds of steam-powered vehicles. It is seen here on a 1930-built 'J Type' Steam Wagon, No. 13536, proudly displayed at a steam fair. The 6 ton wagon is currently painted in the livery of E. & N. Ritchie of Hetton-le-Hole, County Durham.

Part of the attraction of these wonderful machines – apart from the evocative smell – is the strong shapes and patterns they offer to the camera. These details of partially restored Ransomes engine 25542 were photographed in a field at the Haigh Steam & Vintage Fair between Wigan and Bolton in Lancashire.

103

Newcomen's engines were widely used in the mines across Cornwall. The pumping station at East Pool mine has been preserved by the National Trust. This building was erected to house the pumping engine for Mitchell's Shaft at East Pool. It is preserved as part of the mining heritage around Camborne in Cornwall – now a World Heritage Site – and is one of three engines within a mile of the town. Inside is a 30-inch cylinder beam winding engine manufactured in 1887 by Holman's Foundry in Camborne itself. The engine is open to the public having been saved from demolition in 1941, acquired by The National Trust in 1967 and restored to operational standard again in 1975.

INDUSTRIAL ENGINES

According to tradition, one of inventor James Nasmyth's party pieces in the late 1830s was to demonstrate the versatility of his powerful steam hammer. From its invention in 1837, the force imparted by Nasmyth's hammer could be varied with ease, so he would first of all use the hammer to crack an egg in a wineglass leaving the glass undamaged, and after a few adjustments, use the same hammer to strike a blow which caused the entire factory building to shudder.

The hammer was just one of many applications of steam to manufacturing in the first half of the 19th century. Steam power had a huge impact on factory output.

It had been the development of water power which drove the building of the first large factories, but water power was fickle. If the supply dried up, so did the power. Steam was available year-round, as was a steady supply of the coal needed to fire the boilers.

Below: the shells of abandoned engine houses can be found throughout Cornwall - this one is high on the cliffs above the sea at Wheal Coates mine near St Agnes on the north Cornish coast.

Inset: On loan from Heriot-Watt University's collection, this beam engine exhibited at the Scottish Mining Museum is typical of those used to pump water out of deep mines.

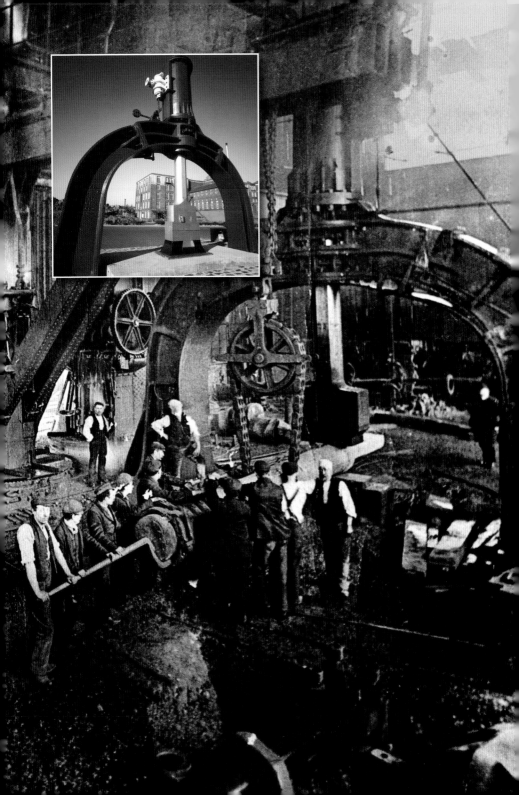

The introduction of powerful steam engines was one of the major innovations which increased industrial output and drove the expansion British manufacturing.

The first practical steam-powered engine was Thomas Newcomen's atmospheric engine, invented in 1712 and subsequently used extensively as a pumping engine to drain coal mines. Newcomen's engine was rather inefficient – some engineering historians rate its efficiency as little more than 1% – but it would be more than half a century before James Watt's condensing engine was successfully demonstrated.

Few of Newcomen's engines have survived, and none in their original locations. Their inefficiency guaranteed their replacement as soon as better engines became available, but one late 18th century example has been preserved and erected in a converted electricity sub-station in his home town of Dartmouth. It is still operational, and open daily to visitors. That particular engine was used as a pumping engine at Griff Colliery in Warwickshire from around 1720.

Opposite: In an unidentified Lancashire factory, a huge metal casting is being shaped with the help of a steam hammer and a team of twelve men

Inset: A steam hammer built in Glasgow by Glen & Ross in 1862 stands in a car park at Wigan Pier.

Claimed to be the world's largest working mill engine, this 2,500hp 4-cylinder triple-expansion engine was built by J & E Wood in 1907 to power the huge Trencherfield cotton mill in Wigan, Lancashire. The engine turned a 26ft diameter drum, feeding power to the mill via 54 ropes. It is still regularly steamed for visitors, but long after this photograph was taken in the 1980s, it was completely rebuilt and has now been repainted in its original green.

An early poster advertising Glasgow's Subway, cable-hauled by static steam engines at various points around the circular route. Until electrified, this was the only cable-hauled underground railway in the world. A recreation of the early system can be seen at Glasgow's Riverside Museum at Pointhouse Quay.

At some time later in the 18th century it was modified and moved to Hawkesbury where it was used as a pumping engine to raise water to feed the higher levels of the Oxford and Coventry Canals. James Watt's first engines were reciprocating engines – ideal for pumping – but the real advance in the use of steam in industry came when Boulton and Watt – who set up their partnership in 1794 – developed the mechanisms for converting the engine's oscillating motion into rotary motion.

That led to the development of steam-powered saws, grinding machines and, of course the huge engines whose rope drums soon drove every large weaving and spinning mill in the world.

Boulton & Watt also built highly efficient beam engines, and their 1812 engine – one of two at Crofton Pumping Station in Wiltshire – is the oldest working example in the world. It pumped water to feed the highest level water pound on the Kennet & Avon canal. Open to visitors in the summer

Belt-driven spinning frames in Robert Owen's New Lanark mills. The mills were originally powered by water from the fast flowing River Clyde, but steam power was first introduced to augment water turbines in 1882. The mills converted to electricity in the 1920s.

A small steam engine preserved as part of the Beamish Open Air Museum in Northumberland.

months and steamed regularly, Crofton is one of the best places to see beam engines at work.

On the A38(M) near Birmingham, an 1817 Boulton & Watt has been re-erected. This was a beam blowing engine, once used in in the blast furnaces at M. W. Grazebrook's Netherton Ironworks. Blowing engines were an essential component in the mass production of iron and steel.

Simple engines soon gave way to double-expansion and triple-expansion engines, greatly increasing efficiency and

To keep the machinery running, ranks of large boilers were constantly fed with fuel. Here, at the Lady Victoria Colliery in Newtongrange, now the Scottish Mining Museum, the 12 Lancashire boilers were fuelled with waste coal dust from the colliery's washeries – the stuff the mine owners could not sell.

The great winding engine at the Lady Victoria Colliery in the Lothians, built by Grant Ritchie & Co of Kilmarnock, was one of the most powerful steam engines in Scotland. It could lift eleven tons.

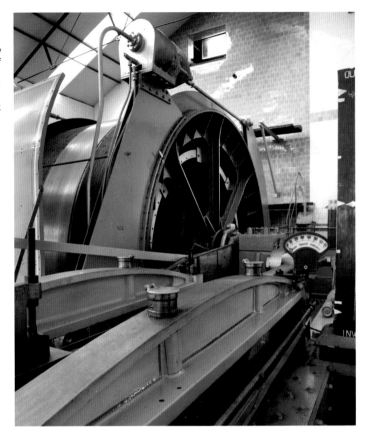

Viewed from above, the huge Lancashire boilers at Lady Victoria, now stripped of their asbestos sheathing, await restoration when funding permits.

power-to-fuel ratios. With the simple engine, the hot steam expanded and cooled very quickly in the cylinder, losing most of its energy before it could be fully utilised.

The multiple engine evolved in 1804 when Arthur Woolf developed a system for harnessing more of the steam's energy in two or more cylinders, avoiding the rapid heating and cooling of the simple engine's cylinder. Woolf's Patent High Pressure Compound Engine was the forerunner of most of the world's most efficient steam engines.

In the compound engine, that steam was fed at high pressure to the first cylinder, then to a second and third cylinder, with expansion continuing through all three, thus utilising much more of its power.

By the 1860s most large mills and factory machines were powered by compound steam engines, steam progressively taking over from water power in older mills.

Steam-powered winding engines were widely used in collieries, creating a pleasing symmetry whereby the coal which fuelled the steam engine was raised out of the ground by that very same engine.

Many of the applications of steam to road and rail transport are mentioned elsewhere in this book, but perhaps two of the most unusual were to be found in Glasgow and Edinburgh. Sadly little evidence remains of either.

The cable system which powered Glasgow's Subway, the world's third underground railway – only London and

This 250hp steam engine, built by Petrie of Rochdale in 1912, was rescued from Philiphaugh Mill near Selkirk, and rebuilt at New Lanark in place of the mill's lost 1882 engine. New Lanark's engines provided ancillary power, with water remaining the main source for the mills. Petrie had built New Lanark's original 550hp engine which also provided heating for the mills.

Seven weavers pose with their looms in the weaving shed at Harle Syke Mill, Burnley, c.1907. This beautifully tinted postcard – part of a series entitled 'Lancashire's Great Industry – shows just ten of the mill's 1,700 looms, all powered by a single large steam engine through ropes and belts.

One of the weaving sheds at John Ryland's Mill in Wigan, photographed c.1904, shows the complexity of the belt-driven system which was powered by the main engine. In a large mill, hundreds of belts on each floor would take power to the spinning, carding, warping and weaving machinery.

Below: The control station at Wigan's Trencherfield Mill with the rope drum beyond.

Budapest were earlier – was installed in 1896 and employed powerful stationary steam engines to drive continuous cable loops around the trackbed of the two circular lines.

Each of the trains was fitted with a clutch system which enabled it to attach and detach itself from the moving cable as required. When the system was modernised in 1935, the gripper and cable system was replaced by a live rail and electric power cars.

Edinburgh's tram system was also cable-driven, with engine houses at various points along the routes. Introduced in 1888, the system remained steam-powered and cable-hauled until electric trams were introduced in 1920. Of course, in company boardrooms across the country, industrial machinery was only worth keeping as long as it was delivering productivity and profitability. So the majority of early factory engines were simply removed and scrapped when their useful lives came to an end.

Where they survived, they did so because there was little or no industrial imperative to replace them with more modern and more expensive engines. That may have been for economic reasons, or because they were so well built that they continued to fulfill their design potential for much longer than might have been originally envisaged.

The machinery in some coal mines, for example, continued to be driven by steam power until the drastic closures of Britain's collieries in the 1970s.

In many other mills and factories, steam was simply replaced by electric power, and the engine houses just locked up and abandoned. From our point of view, those were the lucky ones, for they survived!

They survived due in large part to the enthusiasm of the enginemen who had worked them, and who continued to maintain the machinery even although it was no longer used. In the 1950s when many of these great steam machines were finally pensioned off, heritage and restoration were, for all but a few, ideas which were still far in the future.

A surprisingly large number of steam engines in water and sewage pumping stations have survived, perhaps for no better reason than avoiding the costs of dismantling and disposing of them. Some Victorian pumping stations are cathedrals of engineering achievement, and are now, quite rightly, scheduled monuments. Two of the finest are in London – at Kew Bridge and Crossness.

The Kew Bridge Pumping Station – now known as the Kew Bridge Steam Museum – was built in the 19th century to

Belts driven by the steam engine at Stott Park Bobbin Mill in Cumbria powered not only the lathes, borers and other equipment inside the mill, but also the giant sawmill and winch outside. The mill manufactured millions of wooden bobbins for use in the mills of Lancashire and Yorkshire. In 1880, the water turbine which had powered the mill for many years was replaced by a single cylinder steam engine built by W. Bradley at Gooder Lane Ironworks in Brighouse, Yorkshire. Prior to its move to Stott Park, the engine had worked for 20 years at a Yorkshire coal mine. Since English Heritage took over the site in 1991, Bradley's engine has been beautifully restored to full working order, and is regularly steamed for visitors.

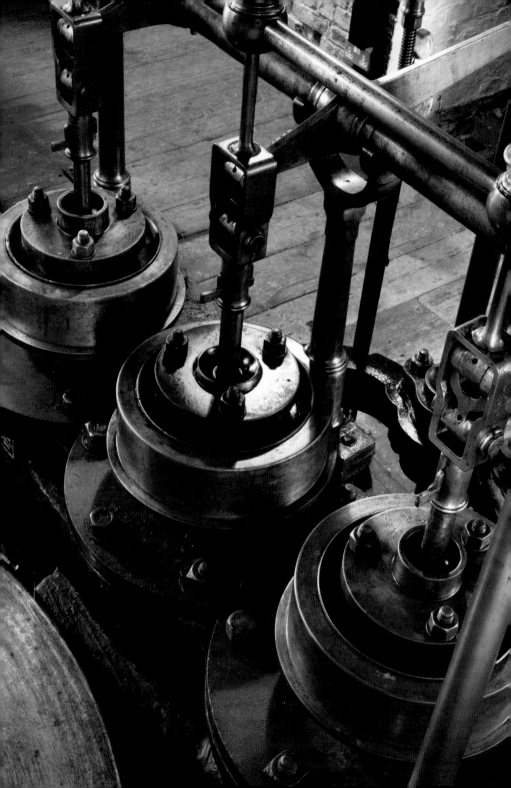

supply London with water. The museum is recognised as the most important historic site to preserve and celebrate Britain's water supply industry. The museum houses what is claimed to be the world's largest collection of Cornish beam engines, amongst them the largest surviving working beam engine, the Grand Junction 90 Engine, which has a cylinder diameter of 90 inches and pumped water to London for just under a hundred years.

The Romanesque style Crossness Beam Engine House, a Grade I listed building, features some of the most spectacular ornamental Victorian cast ironwork surviving today. The four great engines – Prince Consort, Victoria, Albert Edward and Alexandra – have recently undergone extensive restoration by the Crossness Engines Trust.

In Wigan, Trencherfield Mill's huge engines were regularly maintained for some years by former engineman Ted Melling before their first restoration brought them back to steam in the early 1980s. A more recent restoration and complete rebuild in 2009 restored them to their original appearance.

The industrial engine preservation movement is now more than 75 years old. Cornwall's Trevithick Society is one of the oldest industrial preservation societies in the world, having been founded in 1935 to save the Levant beam winding engine from being scrapped. It has since been involved in the rescue and preservation of many of Cornwall's World Heritage Site industrial relics.

Rather younger, founded in 1967, the Ironbridge Gorge Trust oversees a major World Heritage Site in the Severn Valley and has also restored several early steam engines.

But the majority of the restorations of industrial steam engines have been carried out by local groups and trusts determined to preserve key elements of their local histories. The range of skills which these volunteers bring is remarkable. Their enthusiasm and dedication – not to mention their willingness to give their time and expertise freely, has greatly enriched our heritage.

Just a few are still maintained by local authorities – and one such is the Eastney Pumping Station on the edge of Southsea, which is maintained as part of Portsmouth's Museum Service. One of the engines is steamed regularly, and as it is a local authority museum, admission is free.

Opposite: Looking down on to the valve heads of the 42" bore 1812-built Boulton & Watt single acting condensing engine at Crofton in Wiltshire, installed at a cost of £2244 - £600 less than the Sims engine built by Harvey & Co of Hayle, Cornwall which stands along- side it. The engine works a 30 inch pump with a stroke of 7ft pumping 2,500 gallons per minute. It has an efficiency of a mere 1.8%! Extensively rebuilt in 1905, both engines ran until the pumping station was closed in 1959. After a major restoration through the Kennet & Avon Canal Trust, the Boulton & Watt engine was steamed again for the first time in April 1970, and 18 months later the Sims engine returned to steam. 2012 marked the bi-centenary of the Crofton Pumping Station.

Eastney was a sewage pumping station, once capable of pumping over 2.2 million litres of sewage out to sea every hour – but just on a falling tide to make sure it went where it was intended!

On the outskirts of Burton-on-Trent in Staffordshire, the Claymills Victorian Pumping Station, built in 1885, was designed to deal with the same basic problem, and also the growing problem of brewery waste. It operated until 1971. For many years following closure its future looked bleak until its historic importance was recognised.

In 1993 the Claymills Pumping Engines Trust was set up to restore and operate the station. Local volunteers have done virtually all the restoration work and this project really is a good – and thankfully typical – example of just how much a local group can achieve when it decides to preserve something of local and national importance. Today Burton's

JAMES WATT & Cº
LONDON & SOHO BIRMINGHAM
-- 1887 --
LATE BOULTON & WATT.

The two 1886 James Watt & Co two-cylinder engines at Eastney Pumping Station ran at 20 strokes per minute, and could pump over 2.27 million litres each hour. The massive con rods, seen from below ground (opposite) transferred motion from the flywheel to the beam.

Below: looking down on to the heads of the high and low pressure cylinders.

Eastney Engine house, Southsea, was opened in May 1887.

Below: Inside Eastney, the wooden-clad cylinders of the Watt engines can be seen towards the rear of the building. The governors limited the engines to 24rpm. The church-like interiors of many engine houses reflected their role in the quest for purity.

Claymills Victorian Pumping Station stands as one of the largest and probably the most complete remaining Victorian steam pumping stations in Britain.

Claymills also boasts twenty-six other working steam engines which are all original to the operational site.

The large numbers of visitors regularly attracted to the country's engine houses during steaming days attests to the importance of the work that these groups have undertaken. Long may their preservation and restoration work continue.

But keeping these magnificent machines operational requires a great deal of work. As many of our historic engines are housed in listed mill buildings and pumping stations, so the stringent requirements of conservation have to be observed, planned for and, when required, approved by the appropriate heritage authorities.

And nothing is ever straightforward! The requirements of 21st century conservation inevitably involve undoing some of the ill-advised repairs and 'restorations' of well-intentioned volunteers decades ago.

At Crofton Pumping Station on the Kennet & Avon Canal in Wiltshire, the regular maintainance programme occupies much of the closed season, and relies hugely on skilled volunteers. Crofton is unique – the last surviving pumping station still with its original beam engines intact, and still capable of doing the job for which they were installed.

Today, of course, pumping water into the highest reaches of the Kennet & Avon Canal is usually done by electric pumps, but when the beam engines are in steam, the electric pumps are shut down, and 19th century technology resumes the task for which it was installed.

Keeping a two hundred year old pumping station working – Crofton's Boulton & Watt engine celebrated its bicentenary in 2012 – is a labour of love. The teams of volunteers who operate the engine during the open season have usually been developing a work programme based on observing how the machinery operates week by week – and also how the equally-old building stands up to the public footfall during steaming weekends.

Much of the work is routine and happens according to an annual cycle, but with machinery this old, there will inevitably be repairs and replacements to be scheduled into the work programme.

Throughout the closed season, the Crofton volunteers turn up on Tuesdays and alternate Saturdays – different teams according to work commitments – bringing with them the myriad skills needed to keep the place operational. Some are highly skilled retired engineers with a lifetime's experience behind them, while others are steam enthusiasts just happy to help out in whatever way their talents permit.

Amongst the team of volunteers there are carpenters, electricians, a former boiler inspector, bricklayers, and a host of people from non-technical professional backgrounds who just love getting their hands dirty in a good cause. That story, and that range of skills made available voluntarily, is replicated at preserved engines all over the country

Colliery engines required enormous power, not only to raise and lower the heavily laden cages, but also to drive huge ventilating fans which fed air hundreds of feet below the pit yard. This example complete with its rope wheel was salvaged from a Lancashire colliery. The huge power of these fans may have improved the air supply below ground, but the were blamed for the rapid spread of smoke and poisonous fumes from spontaneous underground fires in some collieries.

Lifting one of the exhaust valves on the 1812 Boulton & Watt engine at Crofton Pumping Station during planned maintenance.

Every part of the engine house has a maintenance schedule, especially the boilers and the furnaces. Crofton's current Lancashire boiler came from the Player's factory in Bristol, and has now been operating for well over a century. Typical of the Great Western Railway – who assumed ownership of the Kennet & Avon Canal as early as 1852 – the furnace fronts are emblazoned with the company's name.

The engines continued to pump water long after the canal had ceased to be commercially viable, and the water was used to replenish the boilers of passing GWR railway locomotives.

After the last steaming day of the year, the boiler is given its end-of-season inspection, dried out with warm air, and then sealed up with trays of lime inside to keep it dry. Throughout the building, all bright parts on the engines are covered with 'tarp' which protects them against the corrosive effects of cold damp air throughout the winter.

Then, as the new season approaches, the process is reversed. A month before the first open day, the boiler seals are checked and replaced if necessary, and 3,000 gallons of water are introduced. Then, on the chosen Tuesday, a small fire is lit to warm the machinery. A larger fire is built up on the next day, with a full fire following on the Thursday and, watched by the boiler inspector, a full head of steam is raised. Subject to there being no leaks, Crofton is ready to steam once again!

These procedures, or some very like them, are repeated for every operational steam engine across the country, and it is only the work of these enthusiasts which keeps industrial steam heritage alive and operational. But as costs rise, the challenges they all face become ever more daunting.

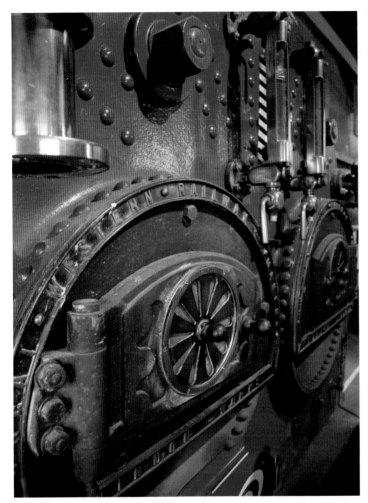

Crofton's Lancashire boilers were purchased secondhand more than a century ago from the Player's factory in Bristol.

The task of fitting replacement ducting inside Crofton's drained 200-year old condenser tank is made more difficult by the lack of working space. A perfect fit is essential.

STEAM RAILWAYS

SCOTLAND

Bo'ness & Kinneil Railway www.srps.org.uk/railway tel: 01506 822298
Bo'ness Station, Union Street, Bo'ness, West Lothian, EH51 9AQ
Operated by the Scottish Railway Preservation Society.
Trains run between Bo'ness and Manuel. Trains steam hauled by historic locomotives. Historic station buildings, open days and special events,

Caledonian Railway www.caledonianrailway.com tel: 01356 622992
The Station, Park Road, Brechin, Angus, DD9 7AF
Reviving an historic name on a 4 mile length of track from the Victorian station at Brechin to Bridge of Dun. Steam trains run on Sundays from Easter to September, diesels at other times.

Royal Deeside Railway www.deeside-railway.co.uk tel: 01330 844416
Milton of Crathes, Banchory, Kincardineshire, AB32 5QH
Operated by The Deeside Railway Company Limited.
A relatively new venture, operated steam trains for the first time in 2010. Limited number of steam days, using Barclay 0-4-0ST *Bon Accord.*

Strathspey Railway www.strathspeyrailway.co.uk tel: 01479 810725
Aviemore Station, Dalfaber Road, Aviemore, Inverness-shire, PH22 1PY
Operated by the Strathspey Railway Company Ltd.
Trains operate on 10 miles of track from Aviemore to Broomhill. With catering on the trains, you can enjoy afternoon tea while being hauled by historic steam locomotives. Open days and shed tours.

CUMBRIA & NORTHUMBERLAND

Lakeside & Haverthwaite Railway www.lakesiderailway.co.uk tel: 01539 531594
Haverthwaite Station, nr Ulverston, Cumbria, LA12 8AL
Operated by Lakeside & Haverthwaite Railway Co. Ltd.
Steam trains run 3.5 miles between Haverthwaite and Lakeside on Windermere. L&HR operates the only preserved Fairburn 2-6-4 tanks.

Beamish Open Air Museum www.beamish.org.uk tel: 0191 370 4000
Beamish Museum, Beamish, County Durham, DH9 0RG
Ride behind replicas of Steam Elephant or Puffing Billy on the Pockerley Waggonway. Steam at the recreated NER Station every weekend from Easter–New Year and occasional live steam on the Colliery Railway system (operating on special events and the first weekend of each month).

Locomotion www.nrm.org.uk tel: 01388 771448
Shildon, Co Durham, DL4 1PQ
The National Railway Museum at Shildon is home to a part of the National Railway Collection, displayed in a superb new exhibition hall. Primarily a museum of classic locomotives, rolling stock and ephemera.

Tanfield Railway www.tanfieldrailway.co.uk tel: 01506 822298
Marley Hill Engine Shed, Old Marley Hill, Gateshead, NE16 5ET
Claiming to be the world's oldest railway, with a trackbed dating in part from 1725! The railway
has an extensive collection of historic industrial locomotives, and steam services operate on most
Sundays.

Weardale Railway www.weardale-railway.org.uk tel: 01388 526203
Stanhope Station, Stanhope, Bishop Auckland, Co. Durham, DL13 2YS
Operated by The Weardale Railway Trust Ltd. The company is reviving one of the oldest branch
lines in the country as a heritage railway. The trust runs weekend steam services from Stanhope
to Bishop Auckland West.

LANCASHIRE & YORKSHIRE

East Lancashire Railway www.east-lancs-rly.co.uk tel: 0161 764 7790
Bury Bolton Street Station, Bolton Street, Bury, Lancashire, BL9 0EY
Operates over a 12 mile track between Heywood and Rawtenstall every weekend and additional
days from May to September. Large collection of locomotives. Open days and steam galas attract
visiting locomotives.

Embsay & Bolton Abbey Railway
www.embsayboltonabbeyrailway.org.uk tel: 01756 710614
Bolton Abbey Station, Bolton Abbey, Skipton, North Yorks, BD23 6AF
Operated by Yorkshire Dales Railway Museum Trust (Holdings) Ltd. Industrial steam locomotives
haul trains between Embsay Station and Bolton Abbey every Sunday and most days in the
summer.

Middleton Railway www.middletonrailway.org.uk tel: 0113 271 0320
The Station, Moor Road, Hunslet, Leeds, LS10 2JQ
Operated by The Middleton Railway Trust Ltd. Industrial steam and diesel locomotives head
trains Saturdays, Sundays, Bank Holiday Mondays and Wednesdays in August. 50th anniversary
in preservation in 2010 and 2012 marks 200 years of revenue earning steam.

Keighley & Worth Valley Railway www.kwvr.co.uk tel: 01535 645214
The Railway Station, Haworth, Keighley, West Yorkshire, BD22 8NJ
Running from Oxenhope to Keighley, this line was rescued immediately after BR closure. With
over 30 locomotives, several of them steamed regularly, the K&WVR remains one of Britain's most
popular railways.

National Railway Museum www.nrm.org.uk tel: 08448 153139
Leeman Road, York, YO26 4XJ
200 years of railway history. The collections include over 100 locomotives, some 250 items of rolling
stock and the most extensive collection of early railway ephemera anywhere in the world.

North Yorkshire Moors Railway www.nymr.co.uk tel: 01751 472508
12 Park Street, Pickering, North Yorkshire, YO18 7AJ
The railway operates an 18-mile line between Pickering and Grosmont, and on specific days, the

24 mile Esk Valley line between Whitby and Battersby via Grosmont where there are engine sheds and a visitor centre.

Ribble Steam Railway
www.ribblesteam.org.uk tel: 01772 728800
Chain Caul Road, Preston, Lancashire, PR2 2PD
The railway has a collection of more than 40 historic industrial locomotives, and steam-hauled services operate on the 1.5 mile track, weekends, April to September. Mainline locomotives on display.

THE MIDLANDS

Churnet Valley Railway
www.churnet-valley-railway.co.uk tel: 01538 360522
Kingsley & Froghall Station, Froghall, Staffordshire, ST10 2HA
Operated by Churnet Valley Railway (1992) plc
Steam services operate on a 10.5 mile line from Froghall to Cheddleton most weekends and Bank Holidays with BR, USA and guest locomotives.

Ecclesbourne Valley Railway
www.e-v-r.com tel: 01629 823076
Wirksworth Stn, Station Road, Coldwell Street, Wirksworth, DE4 4FB
Operated by WyvernRail plc. While the majority of services are diesel, steam-hauled services are run on the 8.5-mile line between Duffield and Ravenstor, the last half mile of which is up a 1 in 27 incline.

Foxfield Light Railway
www.foxfieldrailway.co.uk tel: 01782 396210
Caverswall Road Station, Blythe Bridge, Stoke on Trent, ST11 9BG
A 5.5 mile round trip from Caverswell Road Station to Dilhorne Park on a line originally built to serve Foxfield Colliery. Industrial steam locomotives include Haydock Foundry's 1874-built *Bellerophon*.

Gloucestershire Warwickshire Railway
www.gwsr.com tel: 01242 621405
The Railway Station, Toddington, Gloucs, GL54 5DT
Revelling in the initials 'GWR', the railway operates on 10 miles of track between Toddington and Cheltenham Racecourse, using a mixture of GWR and BR locomotives, including 9F *Black Prince*.

Great Central Railway
www.gcrailway.co.uk tel: 01509 632323
Great Central Station, Great Central Road, Loughborough, LE11 1RW
The Great Central operates an 8 mile section of the former London to Sheffield main line between Loughborough and Leicester, and is the only double-track heritage line in the UK.

Midland Railway Centre
www.midlandrailwaycentre.co.uk tel: 01773 747674
Butterley Station, Ripley, Derbyshire, DE5 3QZ
Both steam and diesel run on the 3.5 mile track from Butterley to Hammersmith. Locomotive sheds and museum at Swanwick, home of the Princess Royal Class Locomotive Trust.

Nene Valley Railway
www.nvr.org.uk tel: 01780 784444
Wansford Station, Stibbington, Peterborough, PE8 6LR
Describing itself as 'the international railway', the NVR has an extensive collection of British, Polish, Swedish and German locomotives, and operates a 5.5 mile line from Peterborough to Yarwell Junction.

Peak Rail www.peakrail.co.uk tel: 01629 580381
Matlock Station, Matlock, Derbyshire, DE4 3NA
An ex-WD J94 regularly hauls trains on 4 miles of track between Rowsley South and Matlock Riverside, on what was once part of the Midland Railway's route from Manchester Central to London St. Pancras.

Severn Valley Railway www.svr.co.uk tel: 01299 403816
The Railway Station, Bewdley, Worcestershire, DY12 1BG
Operates over a 16 mile track carrying more than 250,000 passengers between Bridgenorth and Kidderminster Town, through scenery which captures the essence of a Victorian branch-line.

EAST ANGLIA

North Norfolk Railway www.nnrailway.co.uk tel: 01263 820800
Sheringham Station, Station Approach, Sheringham, Norfolk, NR26 8RA
A 10.5 mile round trip through the Norfolk countryside from Sheringham to Holt, steam-hauled in summer. Steam galas are often boosted by visits from guest locomotives.

THE SOUTH WEST

Bodmin & Wenford Railway www.bodminrailway.co.uk tel: 01208 73555
General Station, Bodmin, Cornwall, PL31 1AQ
From Bodmin Central, the railway operates a 6.5 mile line running north west to Boscarne Junction and south-east to Bodmin Parkway. Trains operate weekends February to December, daily late May to early October.

East Somerset Railway www.eastsomersetrailway.com tel: 01749 880417
Cranmore Station, West Cranmore, Shepton Mallet, Somerset, BA4 4QP
A five mile round trip through the Mendip countryside on the line set up by the artist David Shepherd, starts in the historic station buildings brought to Cranmore from Wells and Westbury-sub-Mendip.

Paignton & Dartmouth Railway www.dartmouthrailriver.co.uk tel: 01803 553760
Queens Park Station, Torbay Rd, Paignton, Devon, TQ4 6AF
The beautiful 7 mile route from Paignton to Kingswear captures the essence of a Great Western branch line. The line operates steam services from April to October plus the usual Santa Specials.

South Devon Railway www.southdevonrailway.co.uk tel: 0843 357 1420
The Station, Dartbridge Road, Buckfastleigh, South Devon, TQ11 0DZ
Running 7 miles from Totnes Littlehempston to Buckfastleigh, the SDR celebrated its 40th anniversary in 2009. Services operate daily from late March until the end of October and on other occasional dates.

Swanage Railway www.swanagerailway.co.uk tel: 01929 425800
Railway Station Approach, Swanage, Dorset, BH19 1HB
Running 6 miles from Swanage, past Corfe Castle, to Norden, steam services hauled by mainline locomotives operate daily from late March to the end of October, plus special weekends and galas.

Swindon & Cricklade Railway   www.swindon-cricklade-railway.org   tel: 01793 771615
Blunsdon Station, Tadpole Lane, Blunsdon, Swindon, SN25 2DA
Currently running from Blunsdon Station to Hayes Knoll, from August 2012 services will be extended to Taw Valley Halt in the Mouldon Hill Country Park. Steam trains run weekends only. The line uses part of the trackbed of the former Midland & South Western Junction Railway.

West Somerset Railway   www.west-somerset-railway.co.uk   tel: 01643 704996
The Railway Station, Minehead, Somerset, TA24 5BG.
20 Miles, 10 stations, and a true GWR branch line experience. Trains run from Bishops Lydeard to Minehead, much of it along spectacular coastline. The S&DR Trust is based at Washford Station.

THE SOUTH EAST

Bluebell Railway   www.bluebell-railway.co.uk   tel: 01825 720800
Sheffield Park Station, East Sussex, TN22 3QL
The 9 mile line from Sheffield Park to Kingscote runs on London Brighton & South Coast Railway trackbed. The Bluebell has the large collection of preserved Southern Railway locomotives .

Buckinghamshire Railway Centre   www.bucksrailcentre.org   tel: 01296 655720
Quainton Road Station, nr Aylesbury, Buckinghamshire, HP22 4BY
A working steam museum on a 25 acre site. Exhibits range from express passenger locomotives to the humble shunting engine. Many of the mainline locomotives are under restoration.

Chinnor & Princes Risborough Railway   www.chinnorrailway.co.uk   tel: 01844 353535
Station Approach, Station Road, Chinnor, Oxfordshire, OX39 4ER
A working railway, with limited steam working, the majority of the trains being diesel-hauled. There are numerous steam days throughout the season, usually with one locomotive in steam.

Didcot Railway Centre   www.didcotrailwaycentre.org.uk   tel: 01235 817200
Didcot, Oxfordshire, OX11 7NJ
Huge collection of GWR locomotives, rolling stock and ephemera. The Didcot collection is said to be the largest collection representing a single company anywhere in the world. Standard gauge and broad gauge.

Kent & East Sussex Railway   www.kesr.org.uk   tel: 01580 765155
Tenterden Town Station, Station Rd, Tenterden, Kent, TN30 6HE
Running 10.5 miles from Tenterden Town to Bodiam, the K&ESR steam-hauled services feature tank engines with Southern Railway or military backgrounds.

Lavender Line   www.lavender-line.co.uk   tel: 01825 750515
Isfield Station, Isfield, Nr Uckfield, East Sussex, TN22 5XB
Steam trains operate most Sundays on a short track between Isfield and Little Horsted. Most steam trains are hauled by one or other of a pair of small saddle tanks.

Mid-Hants Railway   www.watercressline.co.uk   tel: 01962 733810
Station Road, Alresford, Hampshire, SO24 9JG
The Watercress Line runs for 10 miles from New Alresford to Alton. Steam services run most weekends, and daily in summer. Large roster of locomotives from Southern Railways, LMS and BR Southern Region.

Spa Valley Railway   www.spavalleyrailway.co.uk tel: 01892 537715
West Station, Nevill Ter, Royal Tunbridge Wells, Kent, TN2 5QY
Railway runs for 5.25m between Eridge and Tunbridge Wells via Groombridge and High Rocks.
Steam services hauled by a number of locomotive, including ex-LMS 0-6-0T 'Jinty' 47493.

WALES

Gwili Railway   www.gwili-railway.co.uk tel: 01267 238213
Bronwydd Arms Station, Carmarthen, SA33 6HT
The railway operates a short track from Bronwydd to Danycoed and on to Llwyfan Cerrig, and is
the only standard gauge railway operating steam services in South West Wales. 2010 was the line's
150th anniversary.

STEAMBOATS & STEAMSHIPS

HMS *Belfast* (1939)   www.hmsbelfast.iwm.org.uk tel: 0207 940 6300
The Queen's Walk, London, SE1 2JH
Built by Harland & Wolff of Belfast, the 11,553 ton 'Edinburgh Class' cruiser entered service in 1939.
Now part of the Imperial War Museum and moored in the Thames since 1971, she is open daily.

HMY *Britannia* (1953)   www.royalyachtbritannia.co.uk tel: 0131 555 5566
Ocean Terminal, Leith, Edinburgh, EH6 6JJ
The elegant lines of this iconic vessel have been compromised in the cause of visitor comfort, but
in her new berth it is now possible to explore the 5,800 ton John Brown Clyde-built steam turbine
yacht.

SY *Carola* (1898)   www.scottishmaritimemuseum.org tel: 01294 278283
Harbourside, Irvine, Ayrshire, KA12 8QE
Built by Scott & Sons (Bowling) Ltd as the family's private yacht, the 40 ton *Carola* is a rare survival.
Now part the National Historic Fleet, she is undergoing restoration at the Scottish Maritime
Museum.

HMS *Cavalier* (1944)   www.thedockyard.co.uk tel: 01634 823807
The Historic Dockyard, Chatham, Kent, ME4 4TZ
Built in 1944 at Samuel White's Isle of Wight yard, steam turbine-powered *Cavalier* was the Royal
Navy's last operational World War II destroyer. Currently on display at Chatham Naval Dockyard.

ST *Cervia* (1944)   www.thesteammuseum.org/cervia tel: 01227 722502
The Steam Museum Trust, Preston, Canterbury, Kent, CT3 1DH
Cervia is a survivor of a class of World War II tugs built for the the War Ministry, with a massively
powerful triple expansion engine. Currently undergoing restoration in Ramsgate Harbour.

ST *Challenge* (1931)   www.stchallenge.org not currently accessible
The last steam tug to operate on the Thames, *Challenge* is now owned by the Dunkirk Little Ships
Restoration Trust and it is hoped she will return to steam soon. Currently moored in Southampton.

SS *Daniel Adamson* (1903) www.danieladamson.co.uk not currently accessible
A large passenger-carrying tugboat/lighter, *Daniel Adamson* was built as the *Ralph Brocklebank* for the Shropshire Union Canal & Railway Company. She is currently being restored at Ellesmere Port.

RRS *Discovery* (1901) www.rrsdiscovery.com tel: 01382 309060
Discovery Quay, Riverside Dr, Dundee, Angus, DD1 4XA
Now back in drydock in the port in which she was built, Scott's ship on which he sailed to the Antarctic is part restoration, part reconstruction, and fitted out to look as she did on her most famous voyage.

TS *Duke of Lancaster* (1955) not open to the public
Mostyn, North Wales
Embedded in a sand-filled drydock, the former Irish Sea ferry is a reminder of the perils associated with trying to preserve a large steamship and use it for a new purpose. Exterior only is viewable.

HMS *Gannet* (1878) www.thedockyard.co.uk tel: 01634 823807
The Historic Dockyard, Chatham, Kent, ME4 4TZ
The Victorian steam and sail iron-framed sloop is now part of the National Ships Collection, and is preserved at Chatham Dockyard. Built at Sheerness in 1878, and renamed the TS *Mercury* in 1913.

SY *Gondola* (1859) www.nationaltrust.org.uk/gondola tel: 01539 441288
Coniston Pier, Lake Road, Coniston, Cumbria, LA21 8AN
Built by the Furness Railway, the steam yacht *Gondola* has undergone several changed in appearance, emerging as the rebuilt yacht which sails Coniston Water daily between 1 April and 31 October.

SS *Great Britain* (1844) www.ssgreatbritain.org tel: 0117 926 0680
Great Western Dockyard, Gas Ferry Road, Bristol, BS1 6TY
Brunel's great ship, the world's first propeller-driven passenger liner, was rebuilt from the hulk which returned to Bristol in 1970. The project was completed in 2005 and she is open to visitors daily.

PS *John H Amos* (1931) www.medwaymaritimetrust.org.uk tel: 07710 900 004
The Paisley-built *John H Amos* is the last surviving paddle tug in Britain, and is currently undergoing extensive restoration in the Medway. Designed in 1888, the vessel was not launched until 1931, the historically important steamer was already well out of date before she entered the water. The Trust also preserves the steam tug TID 164 (under preservation since 1974, and berthed at Chatham Historic Dockyard) and the Customs cruiser *Vigilant* (currently undergoing restoration at Sheerness).

ST *Kerne* (1913) www.tugkerne.co.uk
Built in Montrose, and now based on the Mersey either at the Liverpool Maritime Museum in Canning Dock or the Ellesmere Port Boat Museum, *Kerne* is currently owned by the North Western Steamship Company Ltd. Access for steamer enthusiasts can be arranged through the website.

PS *Kingswear Castle* (1924)   www.kingswearcastle.co.uk   tel: 01634 827648
Kingswear Castle, The Historic Dockyard, Chatham, ME4 4TQ
Built in Dartmouth, originally for use on the River Dart and now offers trips on the Medway and
Thames each summer. Uniquely, the owners offer courses on every aspect of operating a paddle
steamer.

SS *Lady of the Lake* (1877)   www.ullswater-steamers.co.uk   tel: 01768 482229
Ullswater 'Steamers', The Pier House, Glenridding, Cumbria, CA11 0US
Launched on 26 June 1877, she was designed by Douglas Hebson of Penrith and built in Glasgow
by Joseph Seath & Company. Powered by Kelvin diesels since 1936, but still regularly sailing the
lake.

PS *Maid of the Loch* (1953)   www.maidoftheloch.com   tel: 01389 711865
Loch Lomond Steamship Co, The Pier, Pier Road, Balloch, G83 8QX
The largest paddle steamer ever to sail on Britain's inland waters, and the last ever built on the
Clyde, *Maid of the Loch* is undergoing a restoration programme designed to bring her back into
steam.

PS *Medway Queen* (1924)   www.medwayqueen.co.uk   tel: 01634 575717
Gillingham Pier, Western Arm, Pier Approach Road, Gillingham, Kent, ME7 1RX
Built at Troon in 1924 for the New Medway Steam Packet Company, for work on the River
Medway. Abandoned and sunk in the 1970s, raised in 1987 and currently being rebuilt.

SS *Nomadic* (1911)   www.nomadicpreservationsociety.co.uk
Hamilton Dry Dock, off Queen's Road, Queen's Island, Belfast
Nomadic was built by Harland and Wolff as a tender for the White Star Line liners *Titanic, Olympic*
and *Britannic*. The last of her type, she is undergoing restoration. Exterior only viewable.

SS *Raven* (Windermere) (1871)   www.steamboats.org.uk   tel: 01539 445565
Windermere Steamboat Museum, Rayrigg Road, Windermere, LA23 1BN
Built for the Furness Railway, *Raven* is the only surviving Lakeland cargo steamer. Access restricted
as the museum is currently (2012) closed for redevelopment. Group guided tours, however, can
be arranged.

SS *Raven* (Ullswater) (1889)   www.ullswater-steamers.co.uk   tel: 01768 482229
Ullswater 'Steamers', The Pier House, Glenridding, Cumbria, CA11 0US
Launched on 16 July 1889, she was, like *Lady of the Lake*, built in Glasgow by Joseph Seath &
Company. Powered by Thornycroft diesels since 1934, but still regularly sailing the lake.

SS *Robin* (1890)   www.ssrobin.org
Royal Albert Dock, London
A traditional raised quarterdeck coastal cargo steamer built at the Thames Ironworks, Orchard
House Yard, and powered by a triple-expansion engine by Gourlay of Dundee. The only complete
example in the world of a 19th century coastal cargo steamer. Currently undergoing restoration,
during which time the exterior can be viewed from ExCeL and the Royal Victoria Dock high level
pedestrian bridge.

PS *Ryde* (1937)   not currently open to the public
Binfield, Isle of Wight
Built for the Southern Railway by William Denny & Bros in Dumbarton. Now in a deplorable condition, despite being on the National Ships Register. The Paddle Steamer Ryde Trust is attempting to save her.

SS *Shieldhall* (1955)   www.ss-shieldhall.co.uk tel: 07751 603 190
Berth 29, Southampton Docks, SO14 3XD
Built by Lobnitz & Co. at Renfrew on the Clyde, *Shieldhall* is the largest surviving passenger/cargo steamship in Britain, and she is still sailing regularly. She is still powered by her original triple-expansion engines. Available for cruises and private hire, and bookings can be arranged through the website. A recent financial call for funds to continue her restoration has been well supported.

SS *Sir Walter Scott* (1900)   www.lochkatrine.com/steamship tel: 01877 332000
Trossachs Pier, Loch Katrine, by Callander, Stirling, FK17 8HZ
Much modified since her launch, the steamer still regularly sails the loch. Now fired by bio-fuel, but still with her original 3-cylinder triple expansion steam engine powered by two locomotive-type boilers.

Puffer *VIC 32* (1943)   www.savethepuffer.co.uk tel: 01546 510232
Puffer Steamboat Holidays Ltd, The Change House, Crinan Ferry, Crinan, Lochgilphead, Argyll, PA31 8QH
Now used for summer holiday cruises off Scotland's west coast, *VIC 32* is the last seagoing Clyde Puffer still coal-fired and steam-powered.

Steam Lighter *VIC 96* (1945)   www.vic96.co.uk tel: 01795 892149
The VIC 96 Trust, 29 The Street, Newham, Kent, ME9 0LQ
Victualling Inshore Craft 96 was built in 1945 by Richard Dunston Ltd. of Thorne and was returned to steam in 2009. She is now based in Chatham's No.1 basin, a working exhibit while restoration continues.

HMS *Warrior* (1860)   www.hmswarrior.org tel: 023 9277 8600
Victory Gate, H M Naval Base, Main Road, Portsmouth, PO1 3QX
Britain's only preserved battleship, this pioneering iron-hulled design from 1860 has been almost completely rebuilt, to offer visitors a chance to experience what life on a warship was like 150 years ago.

PS *Waverley* (1947)   www.waverleyexcursions.co.uk tel: 0845 130 4647
Waverley Terminal, 36 Lancefield Quay, Glasgow, G3 8HA
Britain's last sea-going paddle-steamer, *Waverley* is a regular summer sight around Britain's coast. Built on the Clyde by A & J Inglis in 1947, a 2000-2003 refit largely restored her to her 1940s' appearance.

Windermere Steamboat Museum   www.steamboats.org.uk tel: 01539 446139
Windermere Steamboat Museum, Rayrigg Road, Windermere, LA23 1BN
The museum is currently closed to enable the museum's redevelopment – and the restoration of the many boats in the collection, including 1898-built *Kittiwake*. Group tours of the boats can be arranged.

PS *Wingfield Castle* (1934) www.hartlepoolsmaritimeexperience.com tel: 01429 860077
Jackson Dock, Maritime Avenue, Hartlepool, TS24 0XZ
Built in Hartlepool by William Gray & Co, as was her sister *Tattershall Castle*, she was one of three
Humber ferries, and was decommissioned in 1974. She is now preserved as a floating exhibit at
Hartlepool.

TRACTION ENGINE RALLIES

Steam fairs and galas are held throughout Britain each year, from relatively small events featuring
just a few engines in steam, to the absolutely massive annual gatherings such as the Great Dorset
Steam Fair, the Medway Festival of Steam, and others. Magazines such as *Vintage Spirit* publish
annual listings supplements giving dates and contact details for them all. A selection of the major
events is listed on the following pages. Check websites for more details.

Abbey Hill Steam Rally
www.abbeyhillrally.co.uk tel: 01935 891664
Yeovil Showground, Dorchester Road, Yeovil, Somerset
Massive rally, established over 30 years, May Day holiday weekend.

Amberley Museum & Heritage Centre
www.amberleymuseum.co.uk tel: 017982 831370
Old Warden Park, nr Biggleswade, Beds
Live steam events, held in May, June, August and September.

Ardingly Vintage & Classic Vehicle Show
www.ardinglycvshow.org.uk tel: 01273 306817
South of England Showground, Ardingly, West Sussex
Steam engines, steam fairground, etc. over 2 days in July.

Bedfordshire Steam & Country Fayre
www.bseps.org.uk tel: 01462 851711
Old Warden Park, nr Biggleswade, Beds
Three day fair with live steam, held in mid-September.

Belper Steam & Vintage Event
www.belpersteam.co.uk
Street Lane, Denby Village, Ripley, Derbyshire, DE5 8NF
Hundreds of exhibits, working steam, held over 2 days in mid June.

Belvoir Castle Steam Festival
www.steamfestival.co.uk tel: 01780 484630
Belvoir Castle Estate, Woolsthorpe-by-Belvoir, Grantham, Lincs
2-day fair held in May, with hundreds of engines, Victorian fairground etc.

Carrington Traction Engine Rally
no website details
Carrington, near Boston, Lincs
30+ traction engines at 2-day fair held in mid June.

Carters Steam Fairs
www.carterssteamfair.co.uk tel: 01628 822221
Carters organise up to 20 steam fairs, held at venues around London and the south-east between
April and October. See website for details.

Castle Combe Steam and Vintage Rally
www.castlecombesteamrally.co.uk tel: 01454 294117
Castle Combe Racing Circuit, Castle Combe, SN14 7EY
Late May 2-day event established more than 25 years.

Castle Fraser Steam and Vintage Fair
www.bonaccordsteamclub.co.uk
Castle Fraser, by Inveruries, Aberdeenshire, AB51 7LB
2-day fair held in mid June.

Cromford Steam Rally
www.cromford-steam.co.uk
Highacres Farm, Dewey Lane, Brackenfield, Nr Matlock, Derbyshire
Established over 40 years, 2-day event early August.

Deeside Steam & Vintage Rally
no website details tel: 01330 844560
Milton of Crathes, Crathes, Deeside, Scotland
Deeside Steam & Vintage Club annual gathering, late August weekend.

Elvaston Steam Rally
www.elvastonsteam.org.uk tel: 07711 088335
Elvaston Castle Country Park, Station Rd, Borrowash, Derbyshire
Well attended fair, 1st weekend of July.

Essex Country Show
www.essexcountryshow.co.uk tel: 01268 290228
Barleylands, Essex, CM11 2UD
Massive turnout of engines, September weekend after Dorset Show.

Gloucestershire Steam Extravaganza
www.steamextravaganza.com tel: 01453 890891
Kemble Airfield, Cirencester, Gloucestershire
Massive 3-day early August event with hundreds of exhibits.

Grand Henham Steam Rally
www.henhamsteamrally.com tel: 01502 578218
Henham Park, Wangford, Beccles, Suffolk, NR34 8AN
2-day event third weekend of September.

Great Bloxham Vintage Vehicle Show
www.banburysteam.co.uk tel: 01295 320100
Milton Road, Bloxham, Banbury, Oxfordshire
Banbury Steam Society's late-June steamfest over 2 days.

Great Dorset Steam Fair
www.gdsf.co.uk tel: 01258 860361
South Down, Tarrant Hinton, Blandford, Dorset, DT11 8HX
Britain's most famous, and probably largest, steam fair, held over 5 days in late August and early September. Attracts hundreds of participants and thousands of visitors.

Haddenham Steam Rally & Show
www.haddenhamsteamrally.co.uk
Haddenham, nr Ely, Cambridgeshire
2nd weekend of September, hundreds of exhibits.

Harewood Family Steam Weekend
www.harewood.org tel: 0113 218 1010
Harewood House, nr Leeds, LS17 9LG
August Bank Holiday Sunday. Traction engines, steam organs etc.

Honiton Hill Rally
no website details   tel: 01395 516484

Stockland, nr Honiton, Devon, EX14 9NH
Steam and farm vehicles, late August Bank Holiday weekend.

Hunton Steam Gathering
www.huntonsteamgathering.co.uk   tel: 07850 863153

Hunton, Bedale, North Yorkshire, DL8 1QF
2nd weekend of September, with accompanying craft fair. Ploughing match, 20+ steam engines.

Kelsall Steam & Vintage Rally
www.kelsallsteamrally.co.uk   tel: 07739 958294

Churches View Farm, Kelsall Road, Ashton, nr Chester, CH3 8BH
Hundreds of vehicles, many of them steam, over 2 days late June.

Klondyke Mill Preservation Centre Open Day
www.nsctec.co.uk   tel: 0121 353 1050

Klondyke Mill, Draycott-in-the-Clay, Derbshire, DE6 5GZ
A chance to see engine preservation at work, and engines in steam. Event in April, June & October.

Lincolnshire Steam & Vintage Rally
www.lsvr.org   tel: 01507 605937

County Showground, nr Lincoln, LN2 2NA
Established for more than 25 years, late August rally. 1500+ exhibits.

Lingfield Steam & Country Show
www.lingfieldsteamshow.co.uk   tel: 0208 295 1510

Blindley Heath, Surrey
Live steam, static displays and demonstrations, early August.

Llandudno Transport Festival & Victorian Extravaganza
www.llantransfest.co.uk   tel: 01492 545053

Bodafon Fields, Llandudno, North Wales, LL30 1BW
May festival with plenty steam, both stationary and on the streets of the town.

Malpas Yesteryear Rally
www.malpas-yesteryear-rally.co.uk   tel: 01978 780749

Hampton, Malpas, Cheshire
2nd weekend of September 2-day event. 30+ steam engines.

Medway Festival of Steam
www.thedockyard.co.uk   tel: 01634 823807

The Historic Dockyard, Chatham, Kent, ME4 4TZ
Early April gathering. Hundreds of vehicles, steam parades, static displays plus the steamships in the historic dockyards.

Midland Festival of Transport
www.transtarpromotions.com   tel: 01922 643385

Weston Park, Weston under Lizard, Shropshire, TF11 8LE
Early April 2-day event with up to 1500 vehicles, some of them steam.

Norfolk Steam Engine Rally
www.strumpshawsteammuseum.co.uk   tel: 01603 714535

Strumpshaw Hall, Strumpshaw, Norwich, Norfolk, NR13 4HR
50+ steam engines plus lots more. Spring Bank Holiday weekend.

Nottingham Steam & Country Fair
www.midlandeventsclub.co.uk   tel: 01159 135823

Wollaton Park, Nottingham, NG8 2AE
Live steam, static displays and demonstrations, early May.

Preston Steam Rally
www.prestonrally.co.uk tel: 05602 535674
The Steam Museum, Preston Court Farm, nr Wingham, Canterbury, CT3 1DH
Big rally, with nearby steam museum, 2 days late June/early July weekend.

Shrewsbury Steam & Vintage Rally
www.shrewsburysteamrally.co.uk tel: 01743 792731
Shrewsbury, Shropshire, SY3 5EE
This 2-day late August rally attracts over 1000 exhibits.

Somerset Steam Spectacular
www.somersetspectacular.co.uk tel: 01761 470867
Manor Farm, Low Ham, nr Langport, Somerset
3 day event in July, with over 40 working engines.

South Tyne Traction Engine Society Rally
no website details tel: 01434 672253
Tynedale Park, Corbridge, Northumberland
This 2-day mid-June rally was established in the late 1970s.

Steam & Empire Weekend
www.royalgunpowdermills.com tel: 01992 707370
Royal Gunpowder Mills, Beaulieu Drive, Waltham Abbey, EN9 1JY
Award-winning 2-day event held mid-May. One of several live steam events held annually at the gunpowder mills.

Steam in the Park
www.scottishtractionenginesociety.co.uk tel: 01241 860427
Scone Airfield, Perth, Scotland, PH2 6NP
Mid May 2-day rally. One of the biggest traction engine rallies in Scotland.

Stoke Goldington Steam Rally & Fayre
www.stokegoldington-steamrally.co.uk tel: 01908 551330
West Side Farm, Stoke Goldington, Newport Pagnell, Bucks
Well attended steam rally and country fayre. Established 35+ years.

Stradsett Park Vintage Rally
www.nvtec-ea.org.uk tel: 01945 880091
Stradsett Park, nr Downham Market, Norfolk
Stationary steam, vintage machinery, early May.

Tinker's Park Steam Engine Rally
www.tinkerspark.com
Tinker's Park, Hadlow Down, East Sussex, TN22 4HS
40+ engines, and hundreds of vintage vehicles, over two days in early June.

Torbay Steam Fair
www.torbaysteamfair.com tel: 01803 853989
Churston, nr Brixham, Devon
Large 3-day event held in early August.

Ulster Traction Engine Rally
www.ulstersteam.co.uk tel: 07866 555436
The Showgrounds, Ballymena, County Antrim, Northern Ireland
Very large mid-July 2-day fair. Many engines in steam.

Weeting Steam Engine Rally
www.weetingrally.co.uk tel: 01842 810317
Fengate Farm, Weeting, IP27 0QF
Up to 80 traction engines attend for this 2-day event in mid-July.

Westbury Transport & Vintage Gathering   no website details   tel: 01373 864166
Top Field, Bratton Rd, Bratton, Westbury, Wiltshire, BA13 4TT
Late April, 2-day vintage vehicle event with stationary steam engines.

Welland Steam & Country Rally   www.wellandsteamrally.co.uk   tel: 01531 890417
Woodside Farm, Welland, nr Upton-on-Severn, Worcs, WR13 6NG
Established since 1964, this rally takes place over 3 days in late July.

West of England Steam Rally   www.weses.co.uk   tel: 01209 314360
The Showground, Stithians, Truro, Cornwall, TR3 7HL
West of England Steam Engine Society's rally, over 3 days, late August.

Wiltshire Steam & Vintage Rally   www.wapg.co.uk   tel: 01672 512845
Rainscombe Park, Oare, Marlborough, Wilts, SN8 4HZ
2-day event in June staged by Wiltshire Agricultural Preservation Group.

OTHER LIVE STEAM VENUES

In addition to the many rallies and events listed, a number of museums and collections have regular programmes of live steam throughout the summer months, whilst many others have road and farm engines as static exhibits. Some of the venues for live road, farm and fairground steam are listed below.

Dingles Fairground Heritage Centre
www.fairground-heritage.org.uk   tel: 01566 783425
Milford, Lifton, Devon, PL16 0AT
Home of the National Fairground Collection, the museum has a wide range of fairground rides, engines and ephemera. Lots of live steam at the Autumn Fairground Weekend, late September.

Hollycombe Working Steam Museum   www.hollycombe.co.uk   tel: 01428 724900
Iron Hill, Liphook, Hampshire, GU30 7LP
An amazing collection of working steam engines including railway locomotives, farm engines, road engines, maritime engines, and steam fairground rides. Open April to October most weekends, and Weds-Suns in August. 2-day steam rally late May. Check website for details of all steaming dates.

Levens Hall Collection   www.levenshall.co.uk   tel: 01539 560321
Levens Hall, Kendal, Cumbria, LA8 0PD
The traction engines housed at Levens Hall were collected by Robin and Hal Bagot and the collection includes a 1925 Foden Steam Wagon, a 1902 Locke Steam Car, the Fowler 1920 Showman's Road Locomotive *Bertha*, and a half-size Traction Engine, *Little Gem*. Those last two are in steam most Sundays & Bank Holidays throughout the summer season.

Preston Court Steam Museum Collection   www.thesteammuseum.org   tel: 01227 720887
The Steam Museum Trust Ltd, Preston, Canterbury, Kent, CT3 1DH
A huge and expanding collection of all things steam-powered but, surprisingly, only open on steam days and rallies. See website for more precise details.

Scarborough Fair Collection   www.scarboroughfaircollection.com   tel: 01723 586698
Flower of May Holiday Park, Scarborough, North Yorks, YO11 3NU
Huge collection of steam engines and steam-powered fairground rides, assembled by Graham Atkinson, includes some unique survivals of steam lorries – including rare 1908 Foden Steam Wagon – fairground engines etc. Open Wednesday to Sundays April to September, Wednesdays only out of season. Check website for opening times.

Thursford Collection   www.thursford.com   tel: 01328 878 477
Thursford Collection, Thursford, Fakenham, Norfolk, NR21 0AS
Huge collection of steam road and farm engines, plus vintage fairground rides. Claimed to be the largest collection of traction engines in the world. Open April to September, but closed Saturdays.

INDUSTRIAL ENGINES

SCOTLAND

Farme Colliery Engine   www.visitlanarkshire.com/summerlee   tel: 01236 638460
Museum of Scottish Industrial Life, Heritage Way, Coatbridge, ML5 1QD
The 1810 Farme Colliery winding engine, the only surviving example of a rotative Newcomen engine, is currently on display at Summerlee, the site of one of Scotland's most important ironworks.

New Lanark   www.newlanark.org   tel: 01555 661345
New Lanark World Heritage Site, South Lanarkshire, Scotland, ML11 9DB
Robert Owen's superbly restored mills contain a 250hp steam engine, built by Petrie of Rochdale in 1912, rescued from Philiphaugh Mill near Selkirk. Rebuilt at New Lanark in place of the mill's lost 1882 engine.

Prestongrange Beam Engine Museum   www.prestongrange.org   tel: 0131 653 2904
Morison's Haven, Prestonpans, East Lothian, EH32 9RY
A site of major importance in Scotland's industrial history. Includes a Cornish Beam Engine, and Power House unique in Scotland as the only beam engine still on the site where it worked. Free admission.

Scottish Mining Museum   www.scottishminingmuseum.com   tel: 0131 663 7519
Lady Victoria Colliery, Newtongrange, Midlothian, EH22 4QN
The colliery remained steam powered all its working life, and the great winding engine, built by Grant Ritchie & Co of Kilmarnock, was one of the most powerful steam engines in Scotland.

YORKSHIRE & THE NORTH EAST

Abbeydale Industrial Hamlet   www.simt.co.uk/abbeydale   tel: 0114 2367731
Abbeydale Industrial Hamlet, Abbeydale Road South, Sheffield, S7 2QW
Industrial heritage museum in former water-powered tool manufactury. A Davy Brothers steam engine of 1855 which provided auxiliary power survives, but is not currently operational.

Beamish Open Air Musem
www.beamish.org.uk tel: 0191 370 4000

Beamish Museum, Beamish, County Durham, DH9 0RG
The vertical winding engine from Beamish 2nd Pit, built in 1855 in Newcastle, is the sole survivor of a type once common in the North East. Steamed daily in the summer season. Regular displays of road steam engines on at least the first weekend of each month. For special events please see website.

Elsecar Beam Engine
www.elsecar-heritage-centre.co.uk tel: 01226 740203

Elsecar Heritage Centre, Wath Road, Elsecar, South Yorkshire, S74 8HJ
The Elsecar Beam Engine is believed to be the only Newcomen engine still in its original location. There are Open Days throughout the summer season, but otherwise only open by special arrangement.

Kelham Island Museum
www.simt.co.uk/kelham-island-museum tel: 0114 272 2106

Kelham Island Museum, Alma Street (off Corporation Street), Sheffield, S3 8RY
The 12,000 horse power River Don Engine, built by Davy Brothers of Sheffield in 1905, drove Cammell's armour plate rolling mill at the Grimesthorpe Works. One of four built for the purpose, it was moved to Kelham in 1978. It steams Mon-Thurs 12pm and 2pm, and Sunday 12pm, 2pm and 4pm.

Markham Grange Steam Museum
www.markhamgrangesteammuseum.co.uk tel: 01302 330430

Long Lands Lane, Brodsworth, Doncaster, South Yorkshire, DN5 7XD
An interesting collection of steam engines gathered from all over the north of England, lovingly restored by volunteers and regularly steamed. Sunday steaming days each month, plus Bank Holidays.

Ryhope Pumping Station
www.ryhopeengines.org.uk tel: 0191 521 0235

Ryehope Engines Museum, Waterworks Road, Ryhope, Sunderland, SR2 0ND
Ryhope Pumping Station was built in 1868 to supply water to the Sunderland area. It ceased operation in 1967 after 100 years of continuous use. The station's two 100 hp beam engines steamed regularly.

Tees Cottage Pumping Station
www.communigate.co.uk/ne/teescottagepumpingstation tel: 01325 350718

Coniscliffe Road, Darlington, Tees Valley, DL3 8TF
Former Darlington waterworks, now a working museum exploring the history of water supply from steam through to gas and electric pumping engines. Steam and gas engines operate on open days.

Washington 'F' Pit
www.washingtonfpit.org.uk tel: 0191 553 2323

Albany Way, Washington, Tyne & Wear, NE37 1BJ
Victorian steam engine, engine house and headgear, preserved as a monument to Washington's coalmining heritage. The winding engine is now electrically driven. Open seasonally. Free entry.

THE NORTH WEST

Bancroft Mill Engine Museum   www.bancroftmill.org.uk   tel: 01943 602118

Bancroft Mill, Gillians Lane, Barnoldswick, Lancashire, BB18 5QR
A cross compound Corliss valve condensing steam engine made by William Roberts and Son.
It was installed in 1920 and ran until 1978 when the mill was finally closed. A Smith Bros and
Eastwood tandem engine is under reconstruction. Static viewing Saturdays, steaming on 13
selected Sundays.

Bolton Steam Museum   www.nmes.org   tel: 01204 846490

Mornington Road, off Chorley Old Road, Bolton, Lancs, BL1 4EU
More than 30 engines preserved and steamed by the volunteers of the Northern Mill Engine
Society, and housed in their museum next to Morrisons Supermarket. For regular steam days check
website.

Ellenroad Engine House   www.ellenroad.org.uk   tel: 07789 802632

Ellenroad Approach, Elizabethan Way, Newhey, Rochdale, OL16 4LG
The Ellenroad Engine House is all that remains of a huge mill, and it still contains its original
3000hp 1892 engines. A steam-powered beam engine is also on site. The engines are steamed on
the 1st Sunday of each month.

Middleton Top Winding Engine   www.middleton-leawood.org.uk   tel: 01629 823204

Middleton by Wirksworth, Derbyshire
The last survivor of 9 beam winding engines for the Cromford and High Peak Railway Built in
1829 it was used to wind trucks 700ft up and down the 1:8 Middleton Incline. Regular steam days
April to October.

Queen Street Mill Textile Museum   www.lancashire.gov.uk/museums   tel: 01282 412555

Harle Syke, Burnley, BB10 2HX
Queen Street Mill is the only surviving operational steam powered weaving mill in the world. 500
hp tandem compound engine in steam on weekdays and Saturdays (including Bank Holidays)
March to November. See the Tinker Shenton Lancashire boilers and the 308 Lancashire looms still
weaving calico today, powered by the mill's steam engine 'Peace'. Check website for details and
times.

Stott Park Bobbin Mill   www.english-heritage.org.uk   tel: 01539 531087

Finsthwaite, Cumbria, LA12 8AX
Originally water-powered, in 1880 a steam engine was added to augment the water wheel. The
restored 19th century engine is still steamed regularly to power some of the machinery.

Trencherfield Mill Engine House   www.wlct.org/culture/heritage/tmse   tel: 01942 777566

Trencherfield Mill Engine House, Heritage Way, Wigan, WN3 4ES
Built in 1907 to power a massive new spinning mill, this huge J & E Wood horizontal twin tandem
triple expansion engine, developing 2500 horsepower, has recently been beautifully restored back
to its original 1907 appearance, and it is now in steam every Sunday. Admission free.

THE MIDLANDS

Abbey Pumping Station

www.leicester.gov.uk/museums tel: 0116 299 5111

Corporation Road, Leicester, LE4 5PX

Three of the former pumping station's four Woolf compound rotative beam engines, built in Leicester by Gimsons, have been restored back to working condition and are regularly steamed. See website for steaming dates.

Black Country Museum

www.bclm.co.uk tel: 0121 557 9643

Tipton Road, Dudley, West Midlands, DY1 4SQ

In 1986, after more than ten years, the museum completed the construction of a full scale working replica of of Thomas Newcomen's 1712 steam engine – one of his very first successful designs – used for pumping water from coal mines on Lord Dudley's estates. The engine, with a cylinder diameter of 52cm, is steamed regularly throughout the visitor season.

Blists Hill Victorian Town

www.ironbridge.org.uk tel: 01952 433424

Coach Rd, Coalbrookdale, Telford, Shropshire, TF8 7DQ

Part of the Ironbridge Gorge World Heritage Site, steam powered equipment from many locations has been rescued and gathered together. Regular steam weekends through the year.

Claymills Pumping Station

www.claymills.org.uk tel: 01283 509929

Meadow Lane, Stretton, Burton on Trent, Staffs, DE13 0DA

4 Woolf compound rotative beam pumping engines, built in 1885 by Gimson and Co of Leicester, in two separate engine houses with a central boiler house and chimney, are steamed regularly throughout the year.

Coleham Pumping Station

www.shrewsburymuseums.com/coleham tel: 01743 281205

Longden Coleham, Shrewsbury, Shropshire, SY3 7DN

In a building which looks like a non-conformist chapel, this sewage pumping station houses two magnificent Renshaw beam-engines built in 1901. Both the engines are operational on regular 'steam-up' days.

Dogdyke Steam Pumping Station

www.dogdyke.com tel: 01636 707642

Located near Bridge Farm, Tattershall, Lincolnshire, LN4 4JG

The external condensing beam-engine, built by Bradley and Craven of Wakefield in 1856, is possibly the oldest scoop wheel pumping set still regularly steamed in its original location.

Etruria Industrial Museum

www.stoke.gov.uk/museum tel: 01782 233144

Lower Bedford Street, Etruria, Stoke-on-Trent, ST4 7AF

The last surviving steam-powered potters' mill in Britain. The mill is in steam severel times a year when the 1903 boiler is fired and the mill is powered by the 190 year old Georgian beam engine, 'Princess'.

Hereford Waterworks Museum

www.waterworksmuseum.org.uk tel: 0121 557 9643

The Hereford Waterworks, Broomy Hill, Hereford, HR4 0LJ

The oldest working triple-expansion steam pumping engine in the UK stands two-floors high and pumped a million gallons per day. It supplied Hereford with water from 1895 until 1952. Regular 'in steam' open days.

Mill Meece Pumping Station   www.millmeecepumpingstation.co.uk   tel: 01785 617171
Cotes Heath, Near Eccleshall, Staffordshire, ST21 6QU
Two restored 300hp pumping engines, one by Ashton Frost of Blackburn (1914) and the other by Hathorn Davey of Leeds (1927). Static viewing Sundays. Details of steam days can be checked on website.

Nottingham Industrial Museum
www.nottinghamindustrialmuseum.co.uk   tel: 0115 915 3692
Wollaton Hall, Gardens & Deer Park, Wollaton, Nottingham, NG8 2AE
The Basford Beam engine and other static and mobile engines, in steam on the last Sunday of each month. The Nottingham Arkwright Society operates the working engines.

Papplewick Pumping Station   www.papplewickpumpingstation.org.uk   tel: 0115 9632938
Rigg Lane, Ravenshead, Nottingham, NG15 9AJ
Britain's finest Victorian Water Works, the only one in the Midlands to be preserved as a complete working water pumping station. Built 1882-1884. Two 140hp Watt engines in operation during steam weekends.

EAST ANGLIA

Cambridge Museum of Technology   www.museumoftechnology.com   tel: 01223 368650
The Old Pumping Station, Cheddars Lane, Cambridge, CB5 8LD
19th century Pumping Station, where two 1894 Hathorn Davey engines, installed to pump the sewage from the well below the engines to the treatment plant at Milton, are regularly steamed.

Forncett Industrial Steam Museum   www.forncettsteammuseum.com   tel: 01508 488277
Low Road, Forncett St Mary, Norwich, Norfolk, NR16 1JJ
A large collection of industrial engines, including the last inverted vertical triple expansion water-works pumping engine built in the UK. Regularly in steam on the first Sunday of each month, May to November

THE SOUTH EAST

Crossness Pumping Station   www.crossness.org.uk   tel: 020 8311 3711
The Crossness Engines Trust, The Old Works, Belvedere Rd, Abbey Wood, London, SE2 9AQ
The Engine House contains four rotative beam engines – Prince Consort, Victoria, Albert Edward and Alexandra one of which has been restored by the Crossness Engines Trust. Check website for opening times.

Eastney Beam Engine House   www.portsmouthmuseums.co.uk   tel: 02392 827261
Henderson Road, Eastney, Portsmouth, Hampshire, PO4 9JF
An impressive Victorian building containing a pair of James Watt beam engines and pumps, one of which is restored to its original 1887 condition. Open last weekend each month except December.

Kempton Engine House   www.kemptonsteam.org   tel: 01932 765328
Snakey Lane, Hanworth, Middlesex, TW13 6XH
There are several engines on site, operated by the Kempton Great Engines Trust, including the world's largest fully operational triple expansion steam engine - *The Sir William Prescott*. Regular steam weekends.

Kew Bridge Steam Museum
www.kbsm.org   tel: 020 8568 4757
Green Dragon Lane, Brentford, Middlesex, TW8 0EN
A collection of working engines including a 100 inch engine, the largest surviving single cylinder beam engine in the world, built by Harvey & Co of Hayle in 1869. Monthly 'Giants of Steam' steaming weekends.

Markfield Beam Engine & Museum
www.mbeam.org   tel: 01707 873628
Markfield Road, Tottenham, London, N15 4RB
Built by Wood Brothers, of Sowerby Bridge, Yorkshire, between 1886 and 1888, the 100hp engine saw continuous duty operating 2 plunger pumps until around 1905. Check website for steaming dates.

THE SOUTH WEST

Coldharbour Mill
www.coldharbourmill.org.uk   tel: 01884 840960
Uffculme, Cullompton, Devon, EX15 3EE
This 200 year old wool spinning mill contains an 1867 Kittoe & Brotherhood Beam Engine, a rare 1910 Pollit & Wigzell 300hp Steam Engine and a Lancashire boiler. Check website for steam dates.

Crofton Pumping Station
www.croftonbeamengines.org   tel: 01380 721279
Crofton Pumping Station, Crofton, Marlborough, Wiltshire, SN8 3DW
Both the 1812 Boulton and Watt (the world's oldest), and the 1846 Harvey engine are in working condition, and are steamed on several summer weekends from a coal fired Lancashire boiler.

Dartmouth Newcomen Engine
no website details available   tel: 01803 834224
Newcomen Engine House, Mayors Avenue, Dartmouth, Devon, TQ6 9YY
The engine on display was probably built in the late 18th century, and was used to pump water into a canal at Hawkesbury Junction in Warwickshire. Still in working order it was re-sited here in 1963.

East Pool Mine Engines
www.nationaltrust.org.uk   tel: 01209 315027
Pool, near Redruth, Cornwall, TR15 3ED
The pumping engine is one of the largest surviving Cornish beam engines in the world, and the restored winding engine nearby, operated by the National Trust, is in action daily April to October.

Levant Mine & Beam Engine
www.nationaltrust.org.uk   tel: 01736 786156
Trewellard, Pendeen, near St Just, Cornwall, TR19 7SX
In 1935, this the first beam engine in Britain to be privately preserved on its working site. From that grew the Cornish Engine Preservation Society, now the Trevithick Society. The engine is steamed from April to October.

Poldark Mine Engine
www.poldark-mine.co.uk   tel: 01326 573173
Poldark Mine, Wendron, Helston, Cornwall, TR13 0ER
The only Cornish Beam Pumping Engine still pumping water from a mine, albeit now electric-powered. Two other steam engines on site. Poldark Mine was originally known as Wheal Roots.

Westonzoyland Museum of Steam Power and Land Drainage

www.wzlet.org tel: 01275 472385

Hoopers Lane, Westonzoyland, near Bridgwater, Somerset, TA7 0LS
The only surviving pumping station c1830 still working in steam, with all the Grade II* listed buildings still standing. 1861 Easton Amos land drainage machine. A modern shed exhibition hall contains preserved engines. For dates of regular steam events check website.

Index

Page numbers in italics denote illustrations